DREAM

TRAVEL

DREAM

TRAVEL

by Terrill Willson

Terrill Willson

ISBN 1-58500-168-6

About the Book

"Dream Travel" is a book about the phenomenon of out-of-body travel, worlds nonphysical, life after death, inner godmen, spiritual growth and more. The author relates his first and subsequent projections into the etheric dream worlds. Descriptions of the inner planes, what can be seen and done there, how to project into the nonphysical worlds, all are included. Can be consciously experienced and verified by anyone.

TABLE OF CONTENTS

Chapter 1

DREAM TRAVEL OR SOUL TRAVEL

About fifteen years ago I experienced the phenomenon of bilocation for the first time. More out-of-body experiences (OOBE's) were to follow for me.

Unlike today, those early soul-travel adventures of mine often gave me a feeling of separating from my physical body. Springy and energized is how my nonphysical inner body felt, solid to the touch and of the same appearance as my physical form. In my inner body I could think conscious thoughts as well as see objects around me. The big surprise was where I usually ended up. I wanted and expected to project into the physical environment but this seldom happened. Only on rare occasions did I find myself out of body somewhere on Earth. Generally I ended up in some nonphysical world that was solid like my inner body.

Experimenting with different concentration and contemplation techniques gradually improved my success with being able to leave my physical body. Then my OOBE's began to change. Most noticeable was losing the sensation of detaching from my physical self, which is still true for me today. Nowadays when I contemplate in the night or early morning I will drift into sleep and become conscious of already being out of body in a solid inner body. With some degree of consciousness, maybe poor or good, I'll join some inner world for a brief or extended period of time until being drawn back inside my physical self automatically. Returns to my body are also different now. Rather than moving slowly through darkness getting back inside my physical form, which is how my early

OOBE's often ended, today most of my returns are instantaneous. Like the end of a dream, one moment I am consciously active in some inner world and the next moment, bingo, back inside my physical body again. I don't even feel myself cross a linear distance. The speed is amazing.

Comparing my OOBE's then and now, the differences are significant. Because my early projections gave me a feeling of leaving my physical body, those had a profound effect on my thinking. Almost overnight my personality changed because the reality of those bilocations was undeniable. Separating from and later moving back inside my physical body meant that such experiences were not dreams or imaginings. They were real! Here was proof of life after death, that people have inner bodies, that nonphysical worlds exist! Verifying such truths changed me.

Then came experimentation and changes in my contemplations and inner travels. Now when I project out of body in the middle of the night or early morning, I generally will not gain consciousness until after shifting into the inner worlds. Neither do my returns, which have become instantaneous, give me a sense of crossing a distance to reenter my physical form. As a result, most of my present OOBE's have a dreamlike quality afterward. They begin and end like dreams so afterward my mind wants to compare them to dreams. I didn't feel myself leave my physical body or return so maybe it was just a dream. My mind often questions the authenticity of such OOBE's the morning after, regardless of how good my consciousness was while out of body. OOBE's like these do not carry the psychological impact as those which begin and end with movement away from and back into my physical body.

Because of dream similarity is why I have come to

think of my present inner travels as dream travel. Soul travel is a more common reference to bilocation, but dream travel as described here is equally authentic, the shift of an inner body into the inner planes. I just don't feel myself leave my body or return.

There are advantages to dream travel, despite dream similarities. Less time and difficulty are involved, at least for me. Unlike years ago when my soul-travel attempts were lengthy and difficult, the contemplation technique that I am using now and have for a number of years is reliable and does not require extensive time. Also, dream travel is less scary for me than my early OOBE's were. Not being conscious when my inner body shifts into the inner planes neutralizes my fear of leaving my body. Suddenly becoming conscious of already being out of body in some inner world is not scary, whereas consciously feeling myself separate from my physical form can be. As for fun, conscious dream travel offers plenty of this.

Chapter 2

CONTEMPLATION TECHNIQUE

Here is a description of the dream-travel technique I am using now. It works automatically, without having to think about or try to project out of body. Troublesome emotions like fear or anticipation are not a problem, and even without regular use this technique can still be effective.

Sometime in the night or early morning I will usually awaken from sleep, probably with a need to head to the bathroom for bladder relief. Others trying this technique may need to set an alarm clock for waking up in the night. For two reasons I find it advantageous to wake up in the middle of the night or early morning and get out of bed for a short time before making a contemplation effort. First, the objective is to fall asleep while contemplating which is necessary and easier for me after waking from sleep. Second, getting out of bed in the night or early morning, even for a few seconds, arouses my conscious mind and hopefully my desire to want to contemplate. People who sleep with a mate will probably have better luck trying this technique if, after waking in the night, they go back to bed in another quiet room.

After visiting the bathroom in the night or early morning, I will then hop back into bed in my normal sleeping position and do one thing. I try to mentally induce a feeling of tightness at a certain spot inside my head. From a spot approximately two inches in back of the top center of my head, downward along a vertical line several inches into my skull, I try to mentally cause a tightness or tenseness or tingling sensation to develop in that general

4

area. This is not difficult to do nor is there an exactness as to the location of this feeling of tightness; anywhere near this imaginary line is satisfactory. There are several ways to do this. I can close my eyes and rotate my eyeballs upward in my eye sockets until a tightness develops in that certain area within or atop my head. Or I can close my eyes and mentally pull backward on my eyeballs in my eye sockets. Or by closing my eyes and pointing each of my eyeballs inward, like crossing my eyes, this can also cause a tightness to develop in that certain area inside my head. Perhaps the easiest way for me to mentally induce this feeling of tightness is to try and mentally pull downward on that spot about two inches in back of the top center of my head. To do this I will give a gentle mental pull backwards and/or downward on my eyeballs, letting them rotate partially upward to a comfortable angle, and then gently pull downward mentally on that certain spot on top of my head.

Moderate your effort here, though. Do not turn this contemplation technique into mental labor or brain strain. Just a slight tightness anywhere in the general area described, either inside or on top of the skull, is sufficient and can be effective for dream-traveling. If some minutes of experimentation are needed to get on the right contemplation track here, this is normal.

Expect also that this method of contemplation won't go smoothly. The mind will repeatedly forget and lose that tightness or tingling sensation inside the head. When this happens to me, I simply readjust my eyeballs and bring the feeling of tightness back. Trying to maintain that tightness will gradually become easier and more relaxing as time passes.

Now all that's needed is to drift into sleep doing this. If I can fall asleep trying to mentally hold this feeling of tightness inside my head, my chances are good of ending up in some nonphysical world. During an early stage of sleep I will suddenly become conscious of being in a solid inner body in a three-dimensional lifelike environment.

Why this technique works remains a mystery to me, but my guess is that either the pituitary gland or the pineal gland inside the head are somehow affected. These two glands are said to be two of Soul's windows for flight into the inner worlds. Chances of projecting out of body automatically after contemplating like this and falling asleep I would estimate as follows: 5-20 minutes of contemplation--20% chance of success, 20-45 minutes of contemplation--40% chance of success, 45-90 minutes of contemplation--60% chance of success.

For explanation sake, let's assume that you try this method of contemplating and manage to slip into sleep. What happens next? Nothing out of the ordinary may happen, or you may fall asleep to vivid dreams. But you may become conscious, either suddenly or gradually, of being in a solid body in the midst of a lifelike world. Your body will feel energized and look like your physical form, probably clothed or at least partially so. Your consciousness can be poor or good. If good, you will realize that you are apart from your physical form in some nonphysical world. Your surroundings will be solid to the touch and may or may not resemble Earth. People may be present, or perhaps animals or even non-Earthlike beings. Where this world is you likely won't know or find out.

So there it is. You have consciously experienced an OOBE. The better your consciousness, the shorter the adventure is apt to be. It may be brief, perhaps seconds or minutes. The end will probably be sudden; one moment you'll be active and conscious in some inner world and the next moment--thinking from inside your physical head again. Where did your inner body and that other world go? This will be confusing. Much of what you did, said, and saw while out of body you now cannot remember. Only parts of the action are still clear in your mind. This will be disappointing.

Sometimes I am asked, "Aren't you afraid of not being able to return to your physical body?" The answer is no. My physical body automatically draws me back inside it sometime during my OOBE's. A return to your physical body will follow the same pattern and may be either instantaneous or a slow or swift flight through darkness. The big problem with returning to your physical body will not be whether you return but when, probably sooner than you want. Always my OOBE's end too soon. Some are very short.

This is dream travel. Each projection will offer different scenery and action. If there is no feeling of leaving the physical body or returning later, an OOBE like this will suffer a dreamlike stigma afterward.

Chapter 3

PROJECTING OUT OF BODY AGAIN

It took several years of soul-traveling for me to figure out a simple way to leave my body more than once the same night. Other novice or veteran soul-travelers should be able to do the same.

That first OOBE of any given night will require some contemplating and may not be easy to achieve. But imagine that you have accomplished this. Somehow you contemplated and projected out of body and have just returned. Now what to do? Regardless of how you managed to leave your body, or whether you were conscious at the moment of projection, whether the experience lasted for seconds or hours, whether your return was slow, fast, or instantaneous, none of this affects what I am about to describe here. All that matters is that your inner body did shift either to someplace in the physical environment or into some nonphysical plane.

Now the question: How to leave your body again this night? The answer: Remain absolutely, perfectly motionless and fall asleep. If you can do this, your chances of projecting out of body again automatically during sleep are excellent.

Sound too easy? Perhaps, there is a catch. Oftentimes after returning from an OOBE my physical body will feel somewhat numb or uncomfortable. In order to fall asleep again I may have to shift positions in bed. If I do this, move my body even slightly, I will have to contemplate until slipping into sleep in order to project out again.

Two, three, four, five or more back-to-back OOBE's

can be achieved in a night this way, provided a person can lie motionless and fall asleep after each return. While waiting for sleep it is okay to gently swallow if need be, but no other part of the physical body should be moved, not even a finger or toe.

Nothing complicated so far, but what about consciousness? Having good consciousness is what makes soul travel or dream travel fun and exciting. But after returning from a trip out of body, if I simply remain motionless and go to sleep, my consciousness during a successive projection will likely be poor. To enhance my consciousness during repeat OOBE's, I need to direct my attention at something, anything, while remaining motionless waiting for sleep. Usually I will listen inside my head for a faint high whistle although my attention can be aimed at anything else with the same result. After slipping into sleep I will suddenly become conscious of being in a solid inner body in some nonphysical world. I could end up in the same inner-world environment that I was drawn away from earlier.

Chapter 4

INNER WORLDS

Think of a clothed inner body of the same shape and appearance as a physical person, able to see and hear in this physical environment without being visible to human eyes. Most people can imagine out-of-body travel here on Earth, if not believe. Stories of Jesus and others come to mind.

But try to picture nonphysical worlds. These seem fairy-tale to people. Do they really exist? How can they be solid?

A common expectation for beginning soul-travelers is that OOBE's will occur on Earth. Because the physical plane is the lowest among the living worlds, the Earth environment should be a training ground for soul travel. But from what I have found, this is not the case. Most of my OOBE's end up in nonphysical worlds. Inner planes seem to be a more natural habitat for inner bodies to visit. Once in a while I find myself out of body on Earth, but seldom.

Where then are the inner worlds? Where are they located in relation to this Earth world, and what do they look like? What is in them? Are they really solid?

When I first began reading about soul travel, inner worlds, and related spiritual topics, I assumed that the astral plane set on top of the physical plane. The physical world is said to be the lowest of all worlds so the astral plane must be suspended above the physical. Likewise for the causal plane, it must set atop the astral plane. On top of the causal plane must be the mental plane. These are described as the principal planes of existence within the realm of time, space, and matter that soul-travelers can visit and verify.

Slow or rapid movements out of and back into my physical body is how my early OOBE's often started and ended, which gave me a sense of distance. Gliding weightlessly through darkness from one location to another is what it felt like. The physical world and the inner planes seemed to be a distance apart. This fit my idea of what soul travel should be like.

Later my OOBE's began to change. More and more of my projections occurred instantaneously, and my returns the same. Experiences like these did not seem like soul travel afterward; they seemed dreamlike. How can a body move from one location to another without crossing a distance?

More clues were to follow. It happened from time to time, while in bed contemplating or after returning from an OOBE, that I could feel a person touching me (I was sleeping alone). Sometimes during contemplation or at the moment of slipping into sleep I became conscious of hands touching my inner body, perhaps even helping to pull my inner body slowly and gently out of my physical self. Other times after returning from an OOBE I lay motionless and could still feel the touch of a person I had been with moments earlier in some inner world.

What these experiences gave clear evidence of was that the physical world and inner worlds are not separated by linear distance. If I can feel another person from the inner planes touching my inner body while I am still inside my physical form, then the physical and inner worlds must be occupying the same areas of space.

Based upon this evidence, it has become my assumption that the physical world and each of the inner planes are separated by energy intensity rather than linear distance. Nonphysical worlds evidently can and are occupying the same space as the physical world, but each coexists separately. How? Because each inner plane and the physical world vibrate at a different energy intensity. Two physical objects cannot occupy the same area of space, but the astral world vibrates at a higher rate of energy than does the physical and can therefore exist in space where physical objects are. Astral objects are solid within the astral world but pass through physical objects. The same is true for the causal plane. Objects in the causal world vibrate with greater energy than do astral objects and can therefore occupy the same space as astral and physical objects. Causal-world objects feel solid but only within the causal world where energy levels match. Ditto for the mental plane. Apparently all of these inner worlds and the physical plane are solid yet occupy the same areas of space throughout all of space. Because each plane vibrates at a different energy intensity is why they can coexist as separate worlds.

So if nonphysical worlds do exist and are solid, what's in them? What is it like being in them? What can be seen and done there? Many questions can be asked here, so let's address some.

Earthlike Or Non-Earthlike

A majority of the inner worlds that I have seen show at least some resemblance to Earth. Nonphysical cities, buildings, vehicles, landscapes, people, animals, colors, etc., can look exactly like or similar to what is found here on Earth. Differences can be subtle or striking. I have seen people in the inner worlds with noses shaped like carrots. I've flown in my inner body over forests of blue trees through a multicolored sky.

Other inner worlds have no semblance at all to Earth, where the terrain, structures, living beings, everything is different. Sights like these can be spectacular.

Remembering such strange scenery afterward may be difficult, though.

Blackness
There is apparently a zone of blackness that surrounds many of the inner worlds, to the sides, below, and above. Dotted with distant specks of white light, this blackness is nonphysical I believe, not part of the physical world. Oftentimes I've projected out of body and moved through darkness for a short time before suddenly finding myself in the midst of some lighted lifelike environment. From within an inner world there may be no blackness visible in any direction. This is common. But numerous times while flying above some nonphysical terrain I have flown too high and suddenly become enveloped in darkness which I did not see from below.

This expanse of blackness is nothing to fear, though. If lost or afraid while in it, the worst that will happen is that emotional distress will cause an automatic return to the physical body.

Inner Body
Nearly all of my inner travels are done in a solid body that feels energized and mirrors my physical appearance. Being consciously separated from my physical form with no body shape at all has happened to me, but only a few times. None of those OOBE's did I understand afterward. When out of body surrounded by blackness, my inner body will feel solid but may not be visible. This I've experienced often. But if the blackness changes to a lifelike world, which is common, my inner body will then become visible in the light.

From reading I have done, it is my understanding that each person possesses more than one inner body. An inner astral body vibrates at a higher rate of energy than does the physical self and is used to see the astral worlds. A common destination for OOBE's is the astral plane. Inside the astral body is a causal body which vibrates with greater energy than does the astral. The energy of the causal body matches that of the causal plane. Within the causal body is another nonphysical body, the mental body, which has more energy yet. Visits to the mental plane require that body.

As best I can tell, many of my dream travels are still done in my astral body. The astral plane has much to see and is usually the first of the nonphysical planes that soul-travelers and dream-travelers explore.

Consciousness

My consciousness when out of body can range anywhere from none to excellent. Having excellent OOB consciousness is the exception and not the rule, however. More often my consciousness in the inner planes will be somewhere between poor and good.

Having minimal or no consciousness during an OOBE happens frequently to me and is nothing to be discouraged about. Projections like these will seem like active dreams afterward. Evidently the subconscious mind and/or the Soul consciousness do the thinking when OOB consciousness is lacking. Whenever I am out of body with poor or no conscious awareness, I'm busy like a robot going here and there doing this and that. But where my thoughts come from is a question.

Dress

My inner body is usually clothed in the inner worlds, either fully or partially. I can be dressed from top to bottom, from neck to waist, from waist to feet, or in shorts only. Apparently some higher power is somehow responsible for dressing me during my OOBE's.

Ordinarily I do not think to scrutinize my clothing while out of body, but occasionally I will. My shirts and pants are likely to be modern casual wear although not copies of my wardrobe here on Earth.

Being nude in the inner planes happens to me from time to time, and it is interesting that such nudity generally will not cause me much embarrassment. Even if other people are present, whether clothed or not, my urge to cover up may be minimal. The same scenario in this physical world would have me scrambling for clothes.

Conversation

My conversations with other people in the inner planes are nearly always carried on in the English language. I speak only English and assume that other soul-travelers converse in the inner worlds in languages familiar to them. I recall a couple of conscious OOBE's whereby I was able to speak and understand a strange language, but this is rare and still a puzzle to me.

Telepathy

Mental telepathy in the nonphysical worlds is not a difficult trick. When out of body I can transfer my thoughts into the minds of other inner-world people, and they in turn can send silent thoughts to me. To do this I think words and sentences in my mind, like talking silently. Such telepathic messages pass through my mind, in or out, one word at a time in sentence form rather than complete thoughts. Usually when this happens I am out of body in a world of blackness with another person nearby. For example, one night after contemplating and falling asleep I suddenly became conscious of standing in darkness in front of someone touching me. A telepathic message passed through my mind from that other person, "I'll bet you don't know where you're at now." Not feeling threatened,

I sent a silent message back, "I don't know where I'm at but I know I'm in front of you." Seconds later the blackness changed to a lighted room inside an Earthlike building. The fellow behind me became visible and we chatted verbally for a short time before I lost control and returned automatically to my physical self.

When out of body in lifelike inner worlds (not blackness), usually my communication will be verbal rather than telepathic. But there are exceptions. Not long ago in an inner Earthlike setting a female and I were passionately French-kissing. As our tongues circled each other's mouths, we were able to communicate mentally by passing silent words and sentences back and forth through our minds. Lots of fun.

This silent talking can even be done within the physical body. In two similar situations: (1) after contemplating and slipping into a sleep/awake state, or (2) after returning from an OOBE and remaining motionless inside my physical form, I've been able to communicate telepathically while inside my physical self. By speaking silent words and sentences in my mind I have been able to send my thoughts to other inner-world people whom I knew or suspected were nearby, or to some higher God-like power (Spirit). These other inner-world people or higher power will sometimes say or do something to acknowledge my message, or perhaps return a silent message to me.

Here is an example. A few years ago while contemplating at bedtime I fell asleep physically but my conscious mind remained awake. Here was a situation of being both asleep and awake which I had experienced a number of times previously. Realizing that an OOBE opportunity was at hand, I kept still and spoke a silent message in my mind "I want to leave my physical body", hoping that something or someone might hear this plea and be of help. Then something strange started happening; an energy force became noticeable around my head. As the energy began surrounding my head and then my shoulders and back, it increased in strength while moving toward my legs. Curious about what was happening, I kept my fears in check and lay motionless as the energy gradually enveloped my entire body. For perhaps fifteen seconds the intensity of the energy grew steadily. But just before reaching a strength that I could no longer withstand, the energy peaked and maintained that peak strength all around me, as if possessing intelligence and knowing my limits of tolerance.

What kept me calm in this situation was my full consciousness. Assuming that the energy possessed intelligence and knew my situation, why would it harm me? Why fear it? To the contrary, I had mentally asked to leave my physical body and perhaps it would assist me. Next to happen was the energy force lifting me upward. Lying motionless on my stomach, the energy felt something like a large magnet locked onto my back as it began slowly lifting my inner body upward horizontally out of my physical self. Several feet above my bed the energy then slowly rotated me to a vertical standing position in mid air. Through dim light I could see the inside of my sleeping room.

Electrified is how my inner body felt as the force then began moving me around. Without taking a step I was pushed about five feet toward the end of my bed, then turned and pushed about ten feet in the opposite direction, then turned and pushed back to where my physical body lay. Then the energy slowly rotated me in mid air to a horizontal position on my stomach and lowered me back inside my physical form. All this time, perhaps thirty seconds, the energy force remained attached to my back like a giant magnet while controlling my movements.

Once inside my physical body again I remained motionless, waiting to see what would happen next. The energy then released its hold on my back and slowly moved toward and above and away from my head until I could no longer feel it. I was back to being in a sleep/awake state again.

Amazed at this, I still realized the communication and OOBE potential in this situation so again I mentally spoke the words, "I want to leave my physical body." Next a hand pushed on my back and instantly I found myself standing in a solid inner body in a lighted Earthlike environment. Fully conscious, leaning against an open doorway of a building, I glanced around and first took notice of my clothes which were yellow trousers and a red flannel shirt, resembling a physical pair of pants and shirt that I owned then. Facing me was a room with maybe a dozen men and women inside so I walked in and casually conversed with some of them. One woman was familiar to me; I recognized her from some other place. A while later my thoughts wandered to my physical self. How was it doing without me in it? In a flash I was back inside my physical body again. The face of the familiar woman I could still see in my mind but now I didn't know her. My conversations with her and the other people I could no longer remember. Feeling numb and tired at this point, I rolled over to a more comfortable position in bed and was soon asleep.

People And Acquaintances

A majority of my projections into the nonphysical worlds involve being with and communicating with people, of varied ages and ethnic races. Most of the inner-world people I see look Earthlike; only occasionally do they display non-Earthlike or abnormal features. It is not often that I visit inner worlds having strange-looking people, beings, creatures, or animals, but such worlds exist.

Encountering people familiar to me from this physical life during my OOBE's is something I still wonder about.

18

Sometimes I meet and talk with deceased people from Earth in the inner planes whom I consciously recognize. Afterwards I will wonder if they really were who I believed them to be. If I meet a familiar person in the inner planes who is still alive here on Earth, and this does happen with some frequency, the question arises: How can a relative or acquaintance from Earth be with me in the inner planes? Did that individual happen to project out of body during the night, in the dream state or otherwise, and meet with me in some nonphysical world? If so, how does this happen? Who or what arranges it? Or was my relative or friend or acquaintance somehow impersonated in the inner planes by something or someone else, for my learning benefit maybe? Lots of unanswered questions here. I've talked later (here on Earth) to some of these familiar people that I have been out of body with, but only one relative could remember being with me in the dream worlds.

My OOBE's may also include people I recognize--but not from this physical life. This happens to me from time to time, and later if I remember the person's face I will wonder where we met before. During a past life maybe, or a prior OOBE?

Gravity And Flight

I can only assume that physical gravity does not affect the nonphysical worlds, but there must be a gravity pull of some kind in the inner planes. What causes it I cannot explain. But without gravity there I and others would float about weightlessly in the nonphysical worlds which does not happen. The gravity tug on my inner body doesn't feel as strong as that on Earth, however, more like the moon, and can also be altered by thoughts which is interesting.

Levitation and flight become possible in the inner planes because of the mind. For example, when out of body in some inner lifelike environment I can walk around or, if I choose to, fly or levitate myself. Both are easily accomplished, just think and do. But I must continue to think about flying or levitating myself while suspended or in flight or a gravity pull can bring me down. I recall a number of times falling to the ground in some nonphysical world because of forgetting to do this.

Speed is another interesting facet of OOBE flight. Usually my flying speed is rather slow, maybe 5-20 mph, and it is normal for me to want to fly faster. Changing my flying speed is difficult, though. Mental concentration will occasionally enable me to fly faster, but not often.

Passing Through Solid Objects

Another feat of magic in the inner worlds is passing through solid objects. The mind is key to accomplishing this, also.

On Earth a physical body cannot pass through physical objects, of course. But in the inner planes an inner body can move through nonphysical objects that feel solid. The procedure is simple: (1) think about passing through an object, (2) remove all traces of doubt from the mind about not being able to pass through the object, and (3) then doing so, continuing to think about passing through the object while moving through it. Note the second requirement: While thinking about and trying to pass through some inner-world object there can be no trace of doubt in the mind about not succeeding. If there is, the object will remain solid to the touch, except for glass which can bend. Only when all doubts have been erased from the mind can an inner body then be extended into and through a solid nonphysical object like a wall, window, door, or something else. The second requirement is what adds difficulty to this phenomenon.

When I'm successful at this, the difference between the vibration and energy of my inner body and whatever object

I am passing through is very noticeable. My guess is that my thoughts somehow temporarily alter the vibration and energy of either my inner body or the object I'm passing through which allows this to happen.

What about an astral body passing through physical objects? Can an astral body project into the physical environment, and if so, can that astral body pass through physical objects? Evidently yes to both questions. I have been out of body a few times on Earth so I know this is possible. An astral body can visit, see, and move around in the physical realm even though the astral worlds are the natural home for astral bodies (because of matching vibration and energy there). But touching physical objects will be difficult for an astral body because physical objects vibrate at a lower rate of energy than do astral entities. When displaced into the physical environment, an astral body will ordinarily be able to pass through any physical object without hindrance. How an astral body moves through physical objects or from place to place is by thoughts.

Pain

Can an inner body feel pain? The answer is yes, but this won't happen often. Only a handful of my OOBE's over the years have brought me pain.

Let's say that you have projected out of body during the night into some lifelike inner world where circumstances become threatening for you. People armed with weapons are confronting you for some reason. If they shoot their weapons at you, will you feel any pain? Can your inner body be injured?

Even a scary encounter like this one, or one involving aggressive people or creatures, will probably not result in any pain for you. Fear may cause the OOBE or vivid dream to end prematurely, before the attackers do you harm. Or the weapons may be pointed at you but not fired. Or the weapons may be fired at you but miss. Even if projectiles are fired which strike you, after the OOBE you may not remember feeling any pain. Seldom have I consciously felt or later remembered feeling pain during a scary OOBE or dream. But it can happen.

Why people have scary OOBE's or scary dreams is open for debate. Evidently a higher God-like power can contrive threatening inner-world settings, presumably for learning purposes. Scary dreams may caution the subconscious mind about personal fears or weaknesses using symbolic characters. Or there could be past-life activities being relived or reviewed.

Most interesting about this possibility of pain in the inner planes is this. Suppose that you are out of body in the scenario described above. Attackers in some nonphysical world are wielding weapons at you. The attackers shoot projectiles which strike you. Will you feel any pain, and if so, how much? Believe it or not, this depends upon how much fear you feel. If you react with fright, there will be a sharp momentary pain when the projectiles pierce and pass through your inner body. No marks or cuts will scar your inner body, nor will the pain be prolonged. If your fear is reduced, the pain will be proportionately lessened. If you feel no fear at all about being hurt, perhaps because of good OOB consciousness, the projectiles will strike and pass through your inner body but cause you no pain. There is apparently a direct relationship between degree of fear and degree of pain in the nonphysical worlds.

There are other ways that an inner body can feel pain, but such pain will not be lasting nor injurious to an inner body. I can recall instances of falling in the inner planes while flying which caused a momentary pain to my inner body upon impacting the ground. There have also been times when a powerful energy or white light suddenly penetrated through my inner body during an OOBE, causing me a sharp pain. But never have any of these instances of pain lasted long or left me injured.

Returns

Returning from an OOBE is simple and easy to do. Too easy in fact. Just wanting to return, or thinking about the physical self in any way, will nearly always initiate an automatic return. Even thoughts like hoping not to return to the physical body will ordinarily cause this to occur. Most of my conscious inner travels end automatically for this reason, and too soon I might add.

Seldom do my returns today give me a sensation of movement, and the same is true for my projections. The advantage of feeling myself leave and later return to my physical body has already been discussed; such OOBE's do not seem dreamlike afterward. They feel real.

More difficult to understand are instantaneous returns (and projections), which are the pattern for me now. How can it be that one moment I am in a solid inner body consciously witnessing a nonphysical world somewhere and the next moment thinking from inside my physical head again? And by instantaneous I mean just that, the speed of light, seemingly without time for movement. Afterward I will wonder if I really went anywhere. Could it have been just a dream?

Something I've noticed over the years about my projections and returns is this. If I can feel myself separate and move away from my physical body, whether slow or fast, I am more apt to feel my return sometime later. I have done involuntary somersaults out of my physical self into blackness and later returned to my body automatically the same way which was odd. But when my projections are instantaneous, my returns are likely to be the same.

Memory Loss

This nagging problem as been with me since my first trip out of body. Years ago it angered me not being able to remember much about my soul-travel adventures, especially after spending hours trying to leave my body. But gradually I've grown accustomed to it.

What usually happens after returning from an OOBE, regardless of my out-of-body consciousness, is that my memory of the events and details will be partial. Some things I may remember clearly, even conversations. If my OOB consciousness was excellent, I may recall most or all of what happened. But even with very good OOB consciousness, some of the action will likely not be clear in my mind afterward. As if my conscious memory can absorb only so much, part of what happened I will later remember, part will be vague, and the remainder will be absent which could be the bulk of the experience. Poor OOB consciousness can leave little in my memory the next morning.

Unfortunately, there is more bad news to this problem of memory loss. Falling asleep after an out-of-body experience will generally rob even more of the action from my memory; by morning I will recall less, maybe much less. The same is true if I leave my body more than once the same night. Back-to-back OOBE's become increasingly difficult to remember, presumably because of the multitude of things seen and done in the inner planes. The memory apparently oversaturates and cannot retain the flood of sights, conversations, activities, faces, etc. Sadly, the result of this is that in the morning I may recall very little of my nighttime OOBE activity.

Fear

Today I am still afraid to leave my body while conscious, maybe more so than as a beginning soul-traveler. Why? Because of instinctive fear and lack of practice. Within humans is an instinctive fear of death or separation from the physical body which I still feel strongly, despite having been out of body hundreds of times these past years. Lack of practice simply means a different way of soul-traveling for me nowadays. Unlike years ago when my OOBE's often began as noticeable detachments from my physical self, most of my projections today are instantaneous. Because I do not often feel myself leave my physical form anymore, it feels strange and somewhat scary for me when this happens.

The sensation of being in an inner body can also bring anxiety, but this fear will diminish and disappear as more OOBE's are achieved. During my first year of soul-traveling I lost this fear entirely.

Yet another fear can come from meeting up with aggressive people, beings, animals, or creatures in the inner planes. I do not have many such encounters, but from time to time this happens to me. Good OOB consciousness will usually keep me calm because I will realize that inner-world aggressors need not be feared. Few have caused pain to my inner body and none have injured me.

An example of a scary OOBE is as follows. One night after contemplating and falling asleep I suddenly became conscious of standing in what looked like the western plains of the United States. The sky was gray, surrounding me was flat open prairie dotted with shrubbery and sagebrush, and in the distance a herd of black cattle was running in my direction. Elated at finding myself out of body, the environment gave me curiosity as did the distant cattle, perhaps several hundred head, running toward me. What did the cattle signify, if anything, and what was to transpire here? Calmly I stood and watched.

On the herd came, the many hooves pounding into the ground and throwing up a cloud of dust. Hands in my pockets, cocky smile across my face, I could only wonder about the stampeding cattle. Seconds slowly passed. The pounding hooves drew closer and began shaking the ground, echoing louder. Still I stood passive and unafraid, fully conscious and confident of not being harmed. Soon the herd was before me, and then came the moment of impact. But surprise! Instead of knocking me to the ground and trampling me, the cattle raced through me! They were solid; this I could see and feel from the ground shaking and dirt flying from the driving hooves. But the energy of the cattle's bodies felt different from the energy of my inner body. I could actually see and feel the cattle as they raced through me one after another. Whether some higher power somehow altered the energy level of the cattle's bodies before impact so as not to match and strike my inner body, I do not know. But whatever happened, I was not harmed and felt no pain. After the herd had thundered through me I turned and watched them race off into the distance. Amused and chuckling at the sight, I could only ponder the meaning.

If I had run in this situation, perhaps because of poor OOB consciousness, would my fear have brought me harm or pain? Speculation is fun, but I am sure that injury would not have been the outcome. Pain possibly, but not harm.

Soul/Soul Body/Soul Consciousness/Soul Plane

What is Soul? An ancient spiritual teaching describes Soul as light and energy without shape or body, possessing knowledge and thinking capability. The physical body, conscious mind, and the inner bodies are merely coverings for Soul within. No two Souls are the same; each is individual and distinct from all others. Home for all Souls is the Soul plane and planes higher which are nonphysical and above the mental plane. Time, space, and matter apparently do not exist in the Soul plane and higher planes which are eternal, as is Soul. In contrast, the lower worlds, the mental, causal, astral, and physical, are eternal and within the realm of time, space, and matter. For a Soul to enter and/or reside in any of the lower planes, an outer protective body or bodies are needed. This is to protect Soul from the lesser vibration and energy of the lower planes.

Does Soul have consciousness? The conscious and subconscious minds are said to have limited capacity in comparison. The plane of the conscious and subconscious minds is the mental plane. Beyond the mental plane, in the Soul plane and higher planes, the conscious and subconscious minds are no longer attached to Soul. An expanded Soul consciousness does the thinking there.

Have I ever visited the Soul plane in my true bodiless Soul form? In this lifetime I honestly do not know. I can recall a handful of conscious OOBE's over the years whereby I seemingly had no body form at all. But did those projections end up in the Soul plane or somewhere else, maybe the astral plane? I'm not certain.

So if the conscious and subconscious minds are not taken with Soul into the Soul plane, how then can any human mind know what Soul, Soul consciousness, and the Soul plane are like? Good question I say. How is this possible? Perhaps visiting the higher inner planes as Soul allows some filtering of knowledge and experience into the conscious mind via the Soul consciousness. This seems plausible. It may be that spiritually advanced individuals can consciously gain information about Soul in this way.

Dreams

Dreams can apparently be in color or black and white although most of mine seem to be in color.

As ordinary as dreams are, however, they remain a mystery to most people. What are they? Dreams evidently represent communication between the nonphysical and physical worlds, information passing to the physical self (conscious and subconscious minds) from Spirit, Soul, or some other source.

Where dreams occur is easy to figure out. Dreams can be an _observance_ of activity in the inner planes, or _participation_ in activity there. During sleep the blackness between the eyes (Spiritual Eye) can change and give a sleeping person a subconscious or conscious view of activity in the nonphysical planes. Dreams can also be OOBE's; while the conscious mind sleeps, the subconscious mind directs a person's inner-body movements in some inner-world setting. Subconscious dream OOBE's are common for everyone.

What is the purpose or value of dreams? Dreams are said to have multiple benefits. They can serve as mental or emotional stabilizers, like a pressure cap on a teakettle, helping a person cope with stress or problems from this physical life. Dreams can also forecast events or give warning signals of things to come. Past-life karma can be worked out as well, by witnessing or reliving portions of past lives which still influence thinking and behavior today. In addition, dreams can be a time and place for instruction and learning.

So how does dream communication work? Why all the strange abnormalities in dreams? Why do dreams not unfold in ways that are easily understandable to the conscious mind? For these answers I have to rely on reading material. Although dreams are shown to us for our learning or spiritual benefit, dream messages are usually garbled in symbols so as not to reveal too much to the conscious mind. Exposing too much about the past, present, or future could be unsettling for many people. For this reason dreams are generally cloaked in symbols, to be deciphered and understood by the subconscious rather than the conscious mind. In this way the subconscious mind can receive useful information without a person's life being disrupted.

Consciously recognizing dream messages can be done, of course, with some analysis. Keeping a dream journal is a good start. Figuring out what various dream symbols represent is how to ungarble the meaning of dreams. Not surprisingly, there is guesswork involved, and memory loss will be a problem.

Chapter 5

MY STORY

Not until I was an adult did I learn about soul travel. The only bilocation stories I'd heard previously were those about Jesus. Then I read two books, "Eckankar: The Key to Secret Worlds" by Paul Twitchell and "In My Soul I Am Free", and wondered. Could ordinary people really project out of body? Is this possible? Several techniques described in these books soon helped me gain proof.

My first projection resulted from a long concentration session at bedtime which exhausted me and put me to sleep physically, yet left me awake mentally. By placing my thoughts a short distance above the crown of my head, a loud roar developed in my right ear. Then bingo--suddenly I was thinking from a location several feet above the top of my head. Surrounded by blackness with no detectable body shape at all, I could think conscious thoughts and even heard voices nearby.

When this happened, a problem developed. My physical body went limp, as if dead, and rolled toward the open side of the bed. Somehow I realized this without being able to see or feel my physical self. Quickly I decided to return to my body for safety reasons, to prevent it from falling onto the floor below. This I did by imagining my physical senses coming back. Suddenly I was surrounded by my physical body again, thinking from inside my head. Unfortunately, after moving my body to a safe position in head, I tried concentrating again for awhile but was unable to project out a second time that night.

Although brief, that first conscious OOBE proved to be

something of a revelation for me. I didn't broadcast it to anyone for awhile in spite of my excitement, though, mainly because of not being able to explain what had happened.

Then a month later came another out-of-body experience even more dramatic. One evening I concentrated at bedtime for quite awhile and eventually fell asleep, but awoke mentally to something unusual. A pattern of small white-bordered rectangles had formed in the blackness in front of my inner vision. While my physical body lay sleeping I consciously studied the rectangles, each with two small saucers of light inside, one white and the other pale blue. Not knowing what to do next in this sleep/awake situation, I had a feeling that the white and blue circles of light possessed intelligence. Therefore, in hopes of communicating, I spoke a silent sentence in my mind, "I want to leave my physical body." No sooner had these words passed through my mind, a force began pushing me upward. Fully conscious, I started rising toward the ceiling, with vision, in a weightless body that felt solid.

Thrilled and frightened were my feelings in this situation, but seeing the ceiling drawing nearer and nearer dominated my attention. Upwards the force continued pushing me, however, into and through the ceiling! Amazing! I could actually feel my inner body pass through the ceiling. Finding myself in dim light in an unfamiliar room, I mentally raised myself to a vertical standing position at this point and took control of my movements thereafter. The force let go of me. To my left was a wall so on a whim I made a lunging motion toward the wall and easily passed through it. Catching sight of my inner body which looked human, I somehow had on trousers and a long-sleeved shirt (shoes I do not recall). The opposite side of the wall appeared to be the darkened exterior of the building where my physical body lay sleeping, but here my thoughts strayed to my physical self. How was it doing? Was it still alright? The moment these thoughts of my physical form entered my mind, instantly my physical senses were back. Without even feeling myself cross a linear distance, I was back inside my physical body again.

Although the speed of this return was baffling, everything else about this OOBE made sense to me. Vivid in my mind were the details: the rectangles and circles of white and blue light, the force pushing me upward, my inner body separating from my physical self, seeing and feeling my inner body pass through the ceiling, glimpsing my inner body and clothing, the feeling of weightlessness. It was this experience, maybe twenty seconds in length, that changed my view of life and death. Without a doubt there was/is life beyond this physical realm.

A soul-travel enthusiast is what I turned into after this second OOBE. But my extended concentration sessions at bedtime during the weeks ahead, not every night but many nights, netted me nothing. Two months passed before I managed to leave my body again. That night I concentrated for a couple of hours at bedtime before becoming conscious of another pattern of rectangles in the blackness between my eyes. Quickly focusing my inner vision on the rectangles, I felt myself nearing a point of separation due to my near-perfect concentration--then out I went into blackness! A slight suction between my eyes (at the Spiritual Eye) and I was tumbling slowly through darkness in a solid, weightless inner body. Thrilled at being out of body again, I tumbled for several seconds through a vast darkness dotted with distant specks of white light until catching sight of a lighted Earthlike environment beneath me. Descending into a basement-style room of some building, I soon came upon two unfamiliar ladies who could see me. Looking and pointing at me, they began talking. Consciously believing I was someplace on Earth, this surprised and confused me. I should be able to see the two ladies but they should not be able to see me in my astral body. My confusion generated concern. Where was this place? Then a force from behind drew me upwards into and through blackness. Next I felt myself surrounded by my physical body and senses again.

Ecstatic about what had happened, my guess was that I'd been out of body for several minutes. My destination remained a puzzle, though. Where had I projected to, and why? To someplace on Earth or not? Also disappointing was my memory loss. Why, after returning to my physical body, were many of the details of this experience now absent from my memory? Despite having good OOB consciousness, the faces of the two women and their conversation I could no longer remember. Visual details of what the room and building had looked like were now sketchy in my memory. This was irritating.

An unexpected thrill had come from this experience, though, which I had not known or read about before. Descending into the Earthlike room subjected my inner body to a weak gravity pull, but this I soon learned could be changed. Using my thoughts I was able to raise my inner body weightlessly above ground level and float myself in different directions. Remarkable!

A week later came my next series of OOBE's. After a lengthy bedtime concentration attempt I fell asleep mentally drained, but during sleep I became partially conscious of who and where I was. Remembering about soul travel, I sleepily began imagining myself in a weightless body. This caused my inner body to detach and lift upward out of my physical form, except for my head. For some reason my inner-body head remained inside my physical head. Therefore, trying to free myself, I sleepily kicked my inner-body legs upward which tumbled me backwards into darkness.

This night I managed three back-to-back OOBE's which was a thrill. The first began in blackness and soon ended up inside an Earthlike house. There I talked with several people whom I believed were living here on Earth. Obviously my consciousness was not good enough to question how I could talk to Earth people in my inner body. After returning from this adventure through darkness, I went back to sleep trying to feel myself still weightless. During an early stage of sleep my inner body moved into blackness automatically, and then another lifelike setting appeared where people talked to me. A third successive OOBE began the same way and had me flying with arms outstretched over a gorgeous ocean shoreline. Although I believed during each projection that I was somewhere on Earth, this could not have been the case if I was able to talk with other people. Clearly some of my out-of-body thoughts here were conscious and some were not.

Following this trio of OOBE's I began to assume that nonphysical worlds must exist. Paul Twitchell's book "Eckankar: The Key to Secret Worlds" explains much about inner planes which I had previously not paid much attention to. Soul-traveling to places on Earth was my primary interest. This I could visualize. But now the game of soul travel was changing; here I was apparently projecting into nonphysical planes. Why, how, or where these inner worlds were located I could not explain, but consciously witnessing them was certainly enlightening. It was sad that after these latest back-to-back projections my memory of what had happened was poor, but in no way did this dampen my soul-travel enthusiasm. I wanted more, and soon.

The coming weeks and months rewarded me with only an occasional trip out of body, however. Long concentration attempts at bedtime many nights trying different soul-travel techniques brought only a few successes. Several times while concentrating there formed in the blackness in front of my inner view a color picture. By focusing my vision on the picture, I was able to project into the scene whereupon the two-dimensional image became three-dimensional when I joined it. This was new.

Of my OOBE's these months, none ended up on Earth. Each took me to some nonphysical world, maybe Earthlike or not. Unfortunately, no mental technique that proved effective for me showed consistency. Whenever I managed to project out of body using an experimental concentration method, always I would try the same technique again with limited or no luck. For months this pattern continued until another change came about. My mind began to balk at concentrating for long periods of time. Eventually I could not even force my mind to go through any more prolonged concentration sessions. What began happening was this: At bedtime I would lay down and try to concentrate in some manner, but my mind would not cooperate. Willpower did not matter; I would soon fall asleep.

Six months after my first conscious OOBE I'd stopped concentrating at nights. My brain simply would not endure the struggle anymore. Unable to master any concentration technique, I had given up hope of ever becoming an accomplished soul-traveler. My out-of-body memories remained dear to me; I was thankful for gaining an assurance of life after death. But my soul-traveling had apparently ended. The concentration needed to accomplish this I could not do, or so I believed.

Then came my next surprise. One night at bedtime I laid down but couldn't sleep because of thinking about an important upcoming event. After resting for several hours my body was fully relaxed but sleep would not come. Then unexpectedly a color picture began forming on my inner mind screen. My only thoughts while resting had revolved around the coming event, not soul travel. Remaining motionless, I expected the picture to fade away at any moment but recognized the soul-travel potential here.

The picture continued to sharpen, however, showing a couple of houses, green lawns, a sidewalk, and a street. As my excitement grew, the scene began to look familiar. Then it struck me! I knew where this place was! It looked like a city residential area where I grew up as a teen. Studying the picture closely, suddenly a slight suction in the vicinity of my Spiritual Eye sent me into the scene. That quickly I was standing in a solid inner body in the midst of three-dimensional houses.

Fully conscious and trembling with excitement about being out of body again, I immediately began running in the direction of my boyhood home just down the street. Clad only in white boxer shorts, my body looked human but felt energized, light and springy. Swift were my strides, but the passing scenery didn't look right. Seeing my former home, it too did not look right. Evidently this was not the neighborhood on Earth that I believed. Next question: Where was this place?

While running I decided to try flying so I jumped off the ground with my arms outstretched and soared up into the sky. Mentally leveling myself off about fifty feet above the ground, I glided over rows of Earthlike houses and then noticed a man sitting on a porch who looked up at me. Being visible to this man gave me a clue that the environment beneath me was probably not Earth. A distance ahead my flight carried me to the outskirts of the city where the landscape changed. Below me stretching to the horizon were extraordinary cliff formations colored in dazzling shades of brown. Awed by this sight, I mentally guided myself down and landed feet-first among the picturesque rocks. Seconds later while gazing in wonder at the scenery there came a tug on me from behind and above.

36

Quickly I was pulled upward into and through darkness and deposited back inside my physical self.

Gone after this OOBE was my soul-travel discouragement. Projecting out of body while relaxed meant that concentration wasn't needed to induce this phenomenon. This time there had been no mental effort. The answer to relaxed out-of-body travel existed; I only had to find it. I wanted that answer.

Experimenting with different ways of relaxing did not go well for me over the coming weeks, though. I tried relaxing without concentrating or visualizing anything but nothing happened. I tried contemplating on some thought or feeling in a relaxed manner while falling asleep. No results. What I learned from this was that relaxing and keeping a particular thought or feeling in mind is not easy. For some reason my mind wandered repeatedly.

Then the unexpected happened again. Feeling tired one afternoon, I laid down to rest but made a special point not to fall asleep. I only wanted to rest for an hour or so and then do something planned. Maintaining an awareness of who and where I was so as not to drift into sleep, I relaxed for maybe thirty minutes without thinking about soul travel. Suddenly a picture caught my attention in front of my inner view. Focusing on the picture drew it closer, making it larger, and then my inner body momentarily moved inside my physical self. But at that opportune moment when I could have and should have let go, mentally I held back, feeling a trace of fear. It had happened so fast. The picture vanished. Gone was a golden soul-travel opportunity, but I'd learned.

A couple of nights later brought another chance. At bedtime that night I tried relaxing and maintaining an awareness of who and where I was. Nothing happened and I fell asleep, but after waking unexpectedly in the night I decided to try again. Relaxing, gazing at the blackness inside my head and maintaining an awareness of my identity, gradually I drifted into a light sleep. Suddenly I became conscious of a picture on my inner mind screen. Quickly focusing on the picture drew it closer and closer until into the scene I went. Later this night I managed two more projections the same way. All presumably ended up in inner worlds rather than the physical environment. Because my consciousness during each was mediocre, my memory afterward of what I did during those OOBE's was poor. But despite this, my soul-travel excitement was bubbling again. Maybe I had discovered something, finally!

Trying this same pattern of contemplation in the weeks ahead reaped only a few successes for me, though. After gaining several more OOBE's this same way, surprisingly the effectiveness of this contemplation procedure disappeared. At bedtime or in the middle of the night I would relax, gaze at the blackness inside my head, and maintain an awareness of who and where I was. Several times a picture formed on my inner mind screen, enabling me to project into the scene. But then my successes stopped--for a reason. During my contemplations I inadvertently began looking for a picture to form in front of my inner view. This kept me from fully relaxing and slipping into an early stage of sleep. Knowing what the problem was didn't help me avoid or solve it either.

After finally realizing that this latest contemplation procedure was not my ticket to soul-travel success, I started experimenting again with similar relaxation methods. Occasionally I gained an OOBE, but not often. One technique that afforded me some repeat success was drifting into sleep, either at bedtime or after waking in the night, keeping my attention on: (1) gazing at the blackness in front of my inner vision, (2) listening to a faint high whistle which usually became audible inside my head, and

(3) imagining myself in a weightless inner body moving further and further away from my physical self into blackness. Contemplating like this while falling asleep netted me a number of OOBE's, but unfortunately this mental technique lost its effectiveness, too. The reason-- same as before: My emotions of anticipation and apprehension started disrupting my contemplations, preventing me from fully relaxing and slipping into a light sleep.

Frustrated with my slow soul-travel progress after a year of effort, I began to analyze why my contemplations were failing. What I needed to figure out was a soul-travel technique that worked automatically but required no thoughts about my physical body. Thinking about leaving my physical body invariably stirred my emotions of anticipation and apprehension, making it difficult for me to relax and drift into sleep. This I needed to avoid.

Reflecting back on all of my past contemplation and concentration sessions, only one consistency came to mind. Oftentimes a faint high whistle had become audible inside my head. "Eckankar: The Key to Secret Worlds" describes a single note of a flute as being a sound emanating from God which can sometimes be heard inside the head. Previously I had not paid much attention to the whistle in my head, but now I started wondering. Could this sound be important?

I decided to try contemplating specifically on the faint high whistle while drifting into sleep. All other thoughts I would avoid, especially any thoughts about leaving my body. Hopefully this would suppress my disruptive emotions of anticipation and apprehension. I also decided to do my contemplating in the middle of the night rather than at bedtime. Doing this should help me slip into sleep while listening to the whistle.

Here then was my new plan for contemplation. At

bedtime I would go to sleep as usual but awaken in the middle of the night, either by alarm clock or self-suggestion. I would then close my eyes and gaze at blackness until a faint high whistle became audible inside my head. Listening to the whistle while falling asleep would become my objective. If it took two or three hours for me to drift into sleep this way, so be it. I was willing to contemplate like this for an extended time. Whenever my mind wandered, I would simply bring it back and begin listening to the whistle again. Any chance of leaving my body would likely come at the moment of falling asleep, provided I was still listening to the sound in my head at that moment.

What to expect from this contemplation procedure I did not know, but my intentions were to give it a fair trial for a few weeks anyway. Any time and effort sacrificed would be well spent if I could find a way to leave my body regularly.

Surprisingly, my very first attempt using this new technique succeeded. After waking in the night I relaxed and contemplated on the high whistle when it became audible inside my head. Drifting into sleep was not easy, requiring a couple of hours or more due to my mind's repeated wanderings. But eventually my tiredness led to sleep. Suddenly I was conscious of a color picture on my inner mind screen, this one an action scene involving people. Focusing on the picture put me there amidst the activity.

The following night this same thing happened, and again the night after. A journal that I kept reveals that I managed to leave my body about 30 different nights over the next six months, which was a remarkable achievement for me. Many nights during those months I didn't or couldn't contemplate, probably at least half, but seeing reliability in this sound technique was certainly encouraging as well as exciting.

Of my OOBE's during this six-month period, several ended up in the physical environment. Twice after contemplating for a lengthy time in the early morning a strong force rotated my inner body 180 degrees inside my physical form. Then like a coil, back I spun automatically to normal position. One early morning I lifted out of my body and was able to view the inside of my sleeping room. Another night during sleep I floated upward out of my physical self and into a nearby wall which made me think at the time, "So this is what it feels like to be dead."

Some of my inner travels during those months included a controlling force behind me which forcibly moved me from one place to another. I also did some kissing and sensual hand-groping with unfamiliar females in the inner planes which was sexually arousing. Another time while out of body I experienced a sudden powerful surge of energy and white light which momentarily caused me some pain, bringing my OOBE to an end.

One night I met and got romantically involved with a lady in the nonphysical worlds. After returning from that love encounter I went back to sleep contemplating and managed to project out again. This time a controlling force pushed me through blackness to where three young girls were sitting in a lighted circle, ages maybe six, eight, and ten. Although the girls had a human appearance, I looked different. My body felt solid like a human body but was transparent, except for many tiny white stars that glowed within me. Fully conscious, I recognized the girls and felt much love for them as the force pushed me up to them. Reaching out my arms, I embraced all three at the same time. But after being pulled back into my physical form a few seconds later, I no longer knew who the girls were, despite being able to still remember their faces. Contemplating and falling asleep again, I soon became conscious of tumbling weightlessly through blackness. Beside me appeared a small white-glowing object shaped about the size of a loaf of bread. For perhaps fifteen seconds this three-dimensional white object bounced along with me as I tumbled slowly through darkness. Several times I reached out and tried picking it up but each time the white object bounced just beyond my reach, as if possessing intelligence. Then came a quick shift back into my physical form.

As strange as this white-object phenomenon was, even more remarkable was the timing of it. Only a month earlier an acquaintance of mine had described to me a similar experience. During a classroom meditation session this fellow had suddenly found himself tumbling through darkness in a solid body. Beside him appeared a three-dimensional white-glowing object which bounced along with him. Knowing nothing about soul travel, his fright at what was happening caused an abrupt return to his physical body. What the white-glowing object was I never did figure out, nor have I witnessed since.

Seeing progress with my soul-traveling encouraged me to continue reading about this and related spiritual topics. Some of my books discussed a Living Master and an Inner Master. The Living Master is described as a Godman in the flesh. The Inner Master (or Dream Master) is his duplicate in the nonphysical planes. Both are said to give spiritual assistance to people and Souls everywhere.

How a Godman in the flesh and a replica Godman in the inner planes can be linked together, and how such Godmen can be in more than one place at the same time perked my curiosity. Could this be true? During several of my OOBE's I remembered about the Dream Master and asked people in the inner worlds if they knew about him or where he could be located. No luck, initially. But then one night while out of body I quizzed a group of people in an

Earthlike setting about the Inner Master. To my surprise I was led to a modern building not far away. Inside, the Inner Master whom I recognized from pictures walked up to me and greeted me by name, shaking my hand. Then he led me down a hallway to a private room where he spoke to me for awhile. My growing excitement listening to him talk is what ended this OOBE. Afterward I couldn't remember much of the Inner Master's conversation which was a disappointment, but having been with him was still memorable. I intended to ask for him more often during my future OOBE's, to try and learn more about this man and his capabilities.

My contemplations did not get easier as the months passed, though. Two hours or more were commonly needed for me to drift into sleep listening to the whistle. Maybe half of the nights I tried. My chances of success were respectable, about one in three. Experimenting with different ways of viewing the black inner screen didn't lead to any discoveries, but I did learn that the early morning was a productive time of day for soul-traveling. Daylight did not matter; being able to slip into sleep while contemplating was the key to success.

Patterns that had surfaced in my inner travels by this time were as follows. First, when out of body, any thoughts about my physical form would invariably draw me back inside it. Second, the better by OOB consciousness, the shorter my experience usually was because of increased chances of thinking about my physical body. The opposite of this was equally predictable; the poorer my OOB consciousness, the less likelihood of thinking about my physical form and therefore the longer my experience was apt to be. Third, the better my OOB consciousness, the better my recall of the events and details afterward. And fourth, the more OOBE's I managed to achieve in a night, the poorer my memory of each. Presumably this was due to my memory being overloaded with so many things seen and done.

Hoping to shorten my contemplations and make them easier, I continued experimenting with different ways of listening to the high whistle. Two changes proved helpful. I found that by waking in the middle of the night and getting out of bed for a brief time, even a few seconds, my chances for an OOBE were improved. The reason: Getting out of bed after waking from sleep aroused my conscious mind for contemplation. A simple trick to make myself do this was to place my alarm clock a distance from my bed. When the alarm rang in the night I was forced to get up out of bed to turn it off. Then I would sleepily splash some water on my face and also go to the bathroom before hopping back into bed. This left me awake enough to want to contemplate but tired enough to fall asleep again. A second change that I added to my contemplations was rather odd. Rotating my eyeballs upward while listening to the faint high whistle and drifting into sleep enhanced my chances of leaving my body. Why I did not know, but experimentation taught me this. The disadvantage of contemplating with my eyeballs rotated upward was difficulty. Falling asleep like this could take over two hours. But if I could persevere for that length of time, and if I was still listening to the sound in my head and pointing my eyeballs upward when sleep came, my chances of automatically projecting out of body were better than 50%. Contemplating like this was difficult, but the odds of success were good.

They didn't come easy, but my soul-travel adventures over the next half year were terrific. And seeing improvement in my OOB consciousness was encouraging as well. A sampling of those projections reveal some patterns and new phenomena. Leaving my body more than once the same night happened more frequently. There were several times that I talked with friends or family members from Earth in the nonphysical planes which perplexed me afterwards. How can this be? Who were these people? On a few occasions I witnessed blue or white stars while out of body in blackness or during contemplation. I also learned about passing my inner body through solid objects in the inner planes which was fun. More than once I managed to crawl out of my physical form during sleep which was new for me. My flights in the inner worlds I began limiting to within 20 feet or so above ground level because flying higher sometimes enveloped me in darkness. One night I was awakened during sleep by a sequence of pictures flashing on and off my inner mind screen.

I had only one OOBE in the physical environment during this six-month period. One early morning after contemplating and drifting back into sleep I gained enough consciousness to crawl out of my physical body limb by limb. Feeling light and giddy as I stood up beside my bed, I had vision and walked through a closed door nearby before I lost mental control and shifted back inside my physical self.

As for the Dream Master, he showed up in a number of my inner travels these months, sometimes after I called out for him. I could never stay with him for very long, though. What generally happened whenever I found myself out of body with him was that I would begin worrying about returning to my physical body. Thinking about my physical form would usually trigger just such an unwanted return.

One night I felt sick at bedtime and woke in the night feeling worse. After going back to sleep something strange began to happen which reawakened me. A current of energy began funneling into my head and through my body, exiting out my feet. Confident of not being harmed, I remained motionless, letting the energy steadily increase in strength until it felt like a flood of water rushing through me, seemingly cleansing my body. After maybe 10 seconds the energy then began to subside and faded away. Rolling over in bed, I felt much better physically. Waking a couple of hours later for work, I felt fine, even refreshed, with no signs of sickness at all.

Here is another tantalizing story. One night while out of body I was kissing a lady in a nonphysical world when my emotions caused a sudden return to my physical self. Lying motionless inside my physical form, I could still feel a pair of lips actively kissing my lips. Amazed and somewhat humored by this, I kept still and drifted back into sleep minutes later lightly contemplating. Suddenly I was conscious of standing in the same inner world as before, kissing the same female. With excellent consciousness I broke off our kiss and began apologizing to her for having abruptly returned to my physical body earlier. She wasn't interested in conversation, though, and started passionately kissing me again which fueled my emotions and caused another quick shift back inside my physical body. Not moving, I could still feel a pair of lips pressing and rubbing against mine. Out of curiosity, to see what would happen, I moved my physical body which caused the touch of the pair of lips on mine to disappear.

I had other OOBE's during these six months with similar endings. Several involved kissing. Once while sitting in an inner world with a woman resting her head on my shoulder I suddenly shifted back inside my physical self automatically. Lying motionless, I could still feel the weight and touch of the woman's head on my shoulder.

This phenomenon of returning to my physical body and being able to feel body contact from the inner planes, maybe hands touching me or a kiss, still happens to me from time to time. There is an explanation. When in the inner worlds my location can be near or even within the

46

area occupied by my physical body. Nonphysical worlds exist in the space where my physical body is, and I can shift into and consciously experience such inner planes for an extended time. When I project back inside my physical self, somehow my inner body reattaches to my physical form automatically, at the top of my head I believe. After reattachment I can only move my physical body, not my inner body. But because of my inner body being energized, it can remain my dominant body if I remain motionless. This means that my dominant inner body, although inside my physical form, can still be touched by inner-world people. However, when my physical senses return, my physical body becomes my dominant body again whereupon nonphysical people can no longer touch my inner body(s).

This same touching phenomenon can also occur while contemplating, believe it or not. There have been times after falling into a light sleep contemplating when I have become conscious of being touched. What happens here is that relaxed contemplation can gradually energize my inner body inside my physical form. If my inner body becomes my dominant body, it can then be touched by people from the inner worlds. Numerous times after contemplating and slipping into a light sleep I've become conscious of hands either rubbing me or gently lifting my inner body out of my physical self. Being lifted and carried is more common. When this happens, one or more pairs of hands lift me gently by my inner-body hips, so gently that good consciousness is required to detect the touching and movement. If I notice this happening, usually I remain motionless and keep my eyes closed to stay calm and not cause an automatic return to my body. My helper(s) will carry me a short distance through darkness and then place me in a lighted lifelike world, letting go of me. Thereupon I will open my inner-body eyes and move about.

It was at this point in time, two years into my soul-traveling, when another of my monumental OOBE's occurred. One night while flying over a nonphysical Earthlike world I consciously remembered about the Inner Master. Hoping that he could hear me somehow, I called out his name. Immediately a force behind me changed my direction of flight. Curious about this, and noticing a light pressure on the bottoms of my feet, I turned my head and looked back. To my astonishment, flying behind me with arms forward, hands lightly gripping my heels, was a man I had never seen before! Anglo, looking maybe 30-35 years of age, dressed in blue jeans and a red and white checkered shirt, he was also transparent! His body and clothing were clearly visible yet I could also see through him. His hands pressed against my feet were obviously solid, though.

Shock was my first reaction upon seeing this transparent stranger flying behind me. None of my soul-travel books had mentioned anything like this. Then came excitement. What a discovery! Here I was, fully conscious, flying above a nonphysical world with a transparent person flying behind me, guiding me by my heels! Incredible!

Wanting to let this fellow know I'd discovered him, I had to shuffle my feet in his hands to get his attention. Flying along with his head down, he was studying the ground below and didn't see me turn my head. Looking up in surprise, he released my feet and waved when I waved at him, then pointed in a certain direction toward the ground. Assuming that he wanted me to fly where he was pointing, perhaps to find the Inner Master there, I could have said something to this man but did not. Instead I nodded my head as if understanding him (which I did not) and dove down toward the ground in the direction he indicated, leaving him behind. There on the ground I asked some people about the Inner Master but none could help.

The following morning I racked my memory for similar past OOBE's. Instances of flying in the inner planes and being pushed by a controlling force, or being bodily lifted and moved around by a force behind me, gave evidence that the controlling force may have been a person. If so, a host of new questions about soul travel now needed answering. Who were these people? How did they know about me and know where to find me? Were they somehow associated with the Inner Master? How did they get behind me so discreetly? What were their motives or objectives? Now the game of soul travel sported new intrigue. Learning some of these answers was going to be fun and interesting in the coming weeks and months.

The very next night I projected out of body and became conscious of being pushed through a darkened sky. Turning my head, a yellowish transparent outline shaped like an oversized human body glowed faintly in the dark behind me. No clothing or facial features were visible, just a yellowish silhouette with arms, legs, head, and body. Curiously reaching back, I tried touching the silhouette but my hands passed through the arms and wrists which felt energized. Then reaching down to where my feet were-- surprise! Two solid hands were gently cupped around my feet!

A second OOBE this night turned out even more bizarre. After returning to my body and going back to sleep contemplating, I suddenly found myself in a solid body in an Earthlike world. Quickly suspending myself above the ground on my back, I watched to see if anyone would fly up and take hold of my feet. No one did, but there seemed to be a buoyant force under me. Reaching down, I could feel energy beneath me but nothing solid. Then reaching back to where my feet were, lo and behold, a giant pair of invisible hands were molded around my feet! Clasping my hands in the giant hands which felt solid, I pulled myself into a sitting position as the hands became my chair. Then folding my arms across my chest in cocky fashion, I proceeded to point where I wanted to go. Whenever and wherever I pointed, the invisible hands pushed me slowly in that direction about five feet above the ground.

In the months ahead the force behind me more often turned out to be a visible person, however, usually a nontransparent adult whom I did not recognize. About a week after the above two OOBE's I was flying in a nonphysical world and noticed a soft pressure on the bottoms of my feet. Reaching back, I pulled up a nice-looking young lady beside me. Excitedly I began asking her one rapid-fire question after another about who she was and what she was doing flying behind me, etc. Before she could reply, though, my overexcitement caused a return to my physical form.

Patterns regarding these fly-behind people gradually began to emerge. When flying in lifelike inner worlds I could usually count on a person to be flying behind me whose body was nontransparent and solid like mine. That person could be male or female, probably unfamiliar to me, maybe old or young, of any ethnic race although more often a Caucasian adult. Only occasionally did I discover the Inner Master flying behind me. But when out of body flying through darkness, it was more common for a transparent human silhouette to be behind me, maybe blue or yellow or even invisible.

To my disappointment, however, I was not able to learn much about these fly-behind people. They could talk, but frequently my excitement after asking one of them a question caused a premature return to my body, before any reply could be given. Sometimes I received answers that didn't make sense to me. Not always were these helpers willing to provide answers. Some answers I forgot after returning to my body. About the only corroborating information I acquired from these people was that some of them knew about the Inner Master. Aside from this, these fly-behind people remained a mystery to me.

Sad to say, this is still true for me today. Rarely will I fly or levitate myself in the inner planes and not have a person or some kind of transparent body or force behind me or with me. How these people know when or where I want to fly is a good question. Do they read my mind? My guess is yes, but perhaps with difficulty. For example, when out of body I may not be able to fly without first spreading my arms like wings, which can be seen from behind. Mental thoughts alone may not lift me off the ground. And to change my direction of flight, arm movements may be needed which are visible from behind. Obviously these fly-behind people know much about me and where I am. But can they read my thoughts? Maybe not. If I mentally try to fly faster, slower, stop, or turn, I often cannot change my flying speed or direction. I may have to turn my head in flight and give verbal instructions to the person behind me. Fly-behind people can evidently see when I raise my arms to fly, but reading my thoughts seems to be more difficult for them.

As for who or what these fly-behinders are, I am still not sure. They may be a manifestation of Spirit rather than actual people. Numerous times while flying I've experimented by reaching back and tossing aside the hands and person there. Each time, amazingly, another person will materialize out of nothing and be flying behind me with arms forward, hands holding my heels. I have tossed aside a dozen or more people like this in rapid succession. Each will differ in age, appearance, and ethnic race and may be transparent or not. All are helpful, courteous, and non-threatening. Some are tight-lipped. But who they are, what they are, where they come from or reside, how they materialize, what they know and how, what their capabilities and objectives are--these answers I still can only guess at.

About the time of discovering the fly-behind people was when I made another change in my contemplation technique. After waking in the middle of the night or early morning, I would go back to sleep with my attention aimed as follows. First I would induce a feeling of tightness at a certain spot about two inches in back of the top center of my head. By rotating my eyeballs upward and/or mentally pulling downward on that spot, a tightness could be induced there. Although a slight tightness could be effective for me, the tighter I could make that spot, the better. After perhaps thirty minutes of this, I would then change tactics and try to drift into sleep listening to the faint high whistle inside my head while keeping my eyeballs rotated slightly upward in a relaxed manner. Contemplating like this and falling asleep seldom went smoothly for me, maybe stretching beyond two hours. But my odds of success were good if I kept trying, kept retrieving my mind each time it wandered. The key to success here was trying to contemplate at the moment of slipping into sleep.

Inducing a tightness just behind the top center of my head became part of my contemplations after some new soul-travel clues surfaced for me. Gradually it became apparent why my earlier contemplation technique of rotating my eyeballs upward as high as possible was effective. Rotating my eyeballs upward causes a tightness to develop behind the top center of my head.

One night after contemplating and drifting into sleep I became conscious of two hands taking hold of my inner-body hands and pulling me slowly out of my physical form into blackness. Remaining motionless so as not to spoil this OOBE, I then began a descent toward an Earthlike room that I could see far below me. The room had no roof, and soon I was sitting on the floor of the room along with about a dozen other people. Standing in the room were the Inner Master and another red-robed man who looked like a teacher. A tingling sensation on top of my head drew my attention. Reaching up, I touched my finger to a strange X-like incision about an inch or two behind the top center of my head. So sensitive was this spot that placing my finger on it caused a return to my physical body. Although brief, this OOBE proved informative.

Within days came another remarkable experience. After projecting out of body in the night I found myself fully conscious flying in darkness. Able to feel a soft pressure on the bottoms of my feet, I was about to turn my head and look back when a wind came up. Blowing against my direction of flight, the velocity of the wind quickly increased to impressive strength, maybe 75 miles per hour or more. Maintaining my flight balance became so difficult that I kept my head and shoulders aimed directly into the wind, not looking back to see who or what was behind me. Flying in a dark wind tunnel is what it felt like. As the wind pummeled the crown of my head, I got the idea to try and mentally induce a feeling of tightness behind the top center of my head. Mentally pulling downward on that spot, like contemplating, suddenly a small hole maybe an inch or two in diameter opened up there. In rushed the wind, pouring through the hole and through my inner body as well as past me. Never have I felt anything so fantastic, like being electrified with energy, yet without pain. Assuming the wind to be Spirit Itself, maybe purifying or enlightening me, I did not want this sensation to end. Just seconds later my joy turned to dismay, however, when I was moved laterally a short distance through darkness to where the wind velocity was much reduced, maybe 15 mph. Turning my head to see who or what was behind me,

I lost mental control and shifted back inside my physical self. The following morning my first step out of bed nearly gave me a fall because of my body still feeling so energized.

When months passed and the hole on top of my inner-body head did not close, my curiosity grew. Why was the hole there? Was it permanent? During some of my OOBE's I reached up and stuck a finger into the hole to see if it was still open. Poking my finger down inside, empty space was all I could feel. The top of my inner-body head was solid except for the circular hole maybe an inch and a half in diameter, but down inside there was nothing. Neither was there pain. Touching the hole caused me no pain or sensitivity. In fact, a finger check was the only way for me to know if the hole was open.

Within weeks after the hole opened, another phenomenon became evident. During some of my OOBE's I became aware of, and could feel, energy funneling downward into my inner-body head through the hole. Several inches wide, this column of energy penetrated through my hand like tiny pins when I reached up and passed my inner-body hand through it, causing a mild stinging to my hand. Again I assumed this energy to be Spirit.

Yet another discovery accompanied this column-of-energy phenomenon. I soon learned that automatic returns to my physical body could be prevented or delayed. This was new and promising. When out of body, if I kept my attention on the tingling sensation where the energy entered my inner-body head, I would not return to my physical body, even if my thoughts included my physical self. The more tingling or energy I could feel or mentally pull into my inner-body head through the hole, the less susceptible I was to being drawn back inside my physical form automatically. For the first time I realized that automatic endings to OOBE's could be avoided, given the right circumstances.

I also began to experience abnormal vision after the hole opened on my inner-body head. By this I mean that during the daytime I would walk around in my physical body with normal vision, yet also be able to see myself going about my daily activities from a vantage point outside myself. For as long as the hole on top of my inner-body head remained open, this outside point of vision stayed with me. But when that hole closed, my outer view of my daytime physical self faded away.

About nine months after the hole on my inner-body head opened is when it closed. First the hole began to shrink in size; this I noticed over a period of several months. Occasionally during an OOBE I would reach up and stick a finger into the hole to see if it was still there. The diameter of the hole gradually decreased to about a half inch, and the energy funneling into my head there diminished proportionately. Then the hole closed over, at first with a thin membrane-like covering that felt flexible and sensitive to the touch. Several times I considered pushing my inner-body finger through the thin covering to try and reopen the hole but did not because of uncertainty about causing harm. Months went by and the covering over the hole slowly turned solid like the rest of my inner body. The column of energy funneling into my inner-body head became undetectable. No longer could I prevent automatic returns to my physical self. My nighttime OOBE activity declined. Projecting out of body became more difficult for me. It appeared and felt as if I had taken a spiritual and soul-travel step backwards. The hole on top of my inner-body head gave evidence of being a shortcut to the inner worlds, perhaps something greater.

Some new and interesting phenomena came out of my active soul-traveling during those nine months when the hole on my inner-body head was open. A number of times while in bed contemplating I felt hands touch my inner body. This happened to me during sleep as well, becoming conscious of hands holding my inner-body hands or gently lifting or pulling me out of my physical form. While asleep I sometimes became conscious of words or pages of words passing before my inner vision on my inner mind screen. Hearing a voice talking to me in my sleep was another oddity. One of my OOBE's treated me to an exquisite choir of singing voices. On several occasions I consciously witnessed a hole about the size of a dime opening or already open in the blackness in front of my inner view (Spiritual Eye), showing inner-world activity through the hole. A few of my contemplations included a deep humming sound which emanated from inside my head. And once I found myself out of body with an exact duplicate of myself, another person who looked and talked just like me. This I never did figure out.

One evening I did some reading about Soul being a bodiless unit of awareness covered by several outer protective bodies or sheaths. That night in my sleep I became conscious of being in blackness, surrounded by distant specks of white light like outer space. Unlike other OOBE's, however, this time I seemed to have no body form at all. I was me, a separate entity of some kind with vision and thinking capability, but without any detectable shape or body. Even more amazing was my thinking capacity; my mental powers seemed limitless. I even thought to myself at the time, "Hey, I know everything about everything!" Unfortunately, my spell of consciousness was brief before lapsing back into sleep. The next morning my impressive mental powers were gone.

Another memorable OOBE began routinely. During a vivid dream I gained enough consciousness to realize that I was already out of body in a solid dream world. Flying with a girl in my arms, I had difficulty flying in a direction that I wanted to go. Puzzled about this, I then realized that someone must be flying behind me. Turning my head, sure enough, there was the Inner Master, arms forward, hands lightly squeezing my heels. Releasing the girl in my arms (I don't know what happened to her after that, apparently she floated away), I reached back to the Master's hands and pulled him into a standing position beside me, suspended above ground. I then asked in a demanding tone why he had prevented me from flying in my direction of choice. Here my mental control wavered, though, which caused my vision to turn fuzzy gray. Suddenly I was back inside my physical body again. Just that quickly a large still-picture flashed onto my inner mind screen inside my physical head, showing the Inner Master's face in black and white. Fascinated by this, I lay motionless and watched, with my physical eyes closed. Next a voice began speaking to me, not through my ears but from inside my head. Recognizing the Master's voice, I listened for about a full minute as he answered my earlier question. Most of his explanation I understood. When the voice stopped, the picture of the Master's face on my inner mind screen vanished. Then two hands took hold of my inner-body hands which were now inside my physical hands. Although faint, the touching continued until I moved my body to a more comfortable position in bed awhile later.

In the months ahead which stretched into years my dream-traveling continued, although not at the pace as when the hole on top of my inner-body head was open. I learned how to leave my body more than once the same night during those months, by remaining motionless after an OOBE and going back to sleep. The Inner Master I saw only occasionally in the inner planes, not as often as might be expected.

My contemplations remained lengthy, however; two or more hours was still common for me which was discouraging. For this reason I didn't or couldn't contemplate a majority of nights. But when I did, my chances of OOBE success were good. To try and reduce my contemplation time I continued experimenting and learned that inducing and maintaining a feeling of tightness just behind the top center of my head could produce conscious OOBE's. Falling asleep keeping a slight tightness there gave me better than a 50/50 chance of projecting out of body automatically. This contemplation technique required less time, too, usually from 45-90 minutes which was an improvement.

A variation of this technique I also used with moderate success. After waking in the night or early morning and getting out of bed, I would go back to bed and induce as much tightness as possible at that certain spot about an inch or two in back of the top center of my head. The tighter I could mentally make that spot, the better. After doing this for about 30-45 minutes I would then stop contemplating altogether and simply fall asleep. I gained some marvelous OOBE's this way.

I also began doing a short contemplation each night at bedtime as suggested in some of my soul-travel books and discourses. Silently or softly repeating HU, either as a single word HU, or as two letters drawn together H......U......, I would do this for several minutes and then go to sleep. Repeating this word, which is another name for God, is said to invite the assistance of Spirit and the Inner Master in the dream state. My dreams remained colorful and active, involving lots of different people plus the Inner Master now and then.

Time continues to pass and I still do a short repetition of HU at bedtime each night. Sometimes after a few minutes of repeating this word and then falling asleep I will consciously find myself out of body in some dream world. When I take the time to contemplate in the night or early morning, I still rely on the technique described here and in Chapter 2 of this book, that of inducing and maintaining a feeling of tightness behind the top center of my head. Regardless of how much time has elapsed since my last contemplation attempt, my chances for an OOBE will be good. Lack of practice does not matter. This technique continues to be reliable for me.

I can also add here that the early morning hours have become my most productive time of day for dream-traveling. Waking early in the morning and heading for the bathroom before going back to sleep lightly contemplating will probably send me into the inner planes with some degree of consciousness.

Chapter 6

WORKING FOR A LIVING

I was working on riverboats that ply the midwestern U.S. rivers when my soul-traveling began. The work schedule was different; for thirty days straight I lived and worked twelve hours a day on one of many towboats that push barges up and down the inland waterways. Then for the next thirty days I left the boat, free to do whatever. The following month I was back laboring on riverboats again. Because I lived in a motorhome then, much of my free time was spent traveling leisurely around the country, living inexpensively and seeing different sights. Although the riverboat work was a slow grind, the time off was great, and did it fly by.

Prior to riverboating I finished college, worked construction for several years, and decided to do some traveling. Being unmarried gave me the opportunity and the push. Buying a used motorhome, I did some repair work on it and then took to the highway with a meager stash of money saved up. My cash supply only lasted a year, unfortunately, but those months of travel and relaxation were super. I think back on that time with fondness: the freedom and peace of mind, my soul-searching, the many wonderful sights.

Bilocation I first read about while on a riverboat, but it was my weeks away from boats that gave me the time to experiment with different concentration and contemplation techniques, trying to learn this skill. Being able to sleep late on my travel days proved invaluable for me. Credit for my early soul-travel successes goes mainly to my free time, plus my desire. Gradually my soul-traveling changed to dream travel.

Then came the time to leave riverboats, after six years. Working six hours on, six hours off, six hours on, six hours off, continually for thirty days straight on a confined towboat didn't offer much for pleasure or career. A change was needed. With money in the bank I started traveling again, semi-retired as I called myself, spending only for necessities. Again I experienced the freedom and peace of mind of a relaxed time schedule. My contemplations and dream-traveling continued with good pace.

Eventually my finances began to dwindle, though, which meant one thing. A job hunt started. More cash was needed. My semi-retirement had come to an end. What kind of job would I enjoy and do well at?

I did go back to work, eight hours a day, five days a week, fifty weeks a year. After a couple of years I made a job change which suited me better. Still single and living in a motorhome, I have sufficient income now but at a sacrifice of free time. It is amazing to see how much of my life is consumed by a full-time job. If I was married and had children, would there be any free time at all?

Yes, my dream-traveling has been affected by my current employment. Less free time adds up to fewer contemplations. Fewer contemplations means fewer OOBE's. Oftentimes I don't have the time or take the time to contemplate for any length of time in the middle of the night or early morning. Not being able to sleep late in the mornings makes a big difference.

But those nights when I do put forth a worthy contemplation effort, my OOBE chances remain good. And I still do a short repetition of HU at bedtime each evening, which keeps my dreams entertaining.

Chapter 7

POTPOURRI

I Am God!

This happened to me some years ago. While out of body one night I was drawn away from a lifelike world into blackness by a force behind me. Moving through darkness at slow speed, I assumed my destination to be my physical body. Wanting to avoid this, I placed my attention on the weightlessness of my inner body and tried holding this feeling in my mind. My movement through blackness slowed to a near-stop, then picked up again, giving me a sense of nearing and then leaving the vicinity of my physical body. This was my hope.

Next came a surprise. A deep voice began speaking, definitely not mine but seemingly coming from within me. The voice began by saying "I am God!" and continued for about three more sentences in this deep God-like tone. Remembering this phenomenon from one of my soul-travel books ("Eckankar: The Key to Secret Worlds"), my best recollection was that this was not God speaking. I therefore interrupted the voice and spoke outloud something to the effect, "No you are not God. Who are you?" After making this challenging statement I was sorry about having done so, however, because the voice stopped speaking and said no more.

A few seconds later the blackness around me changed to a lighted environment resembling Earth. People were present, and a comment I still recall from that gathering was my question to a fellow about where we were. His reply, "The astral plane."

S-t-r-e-t-c-h

Some astral-projection books describe how arms and legs of an inner body can undergo stretching in the nonphysical worlds, without pain or injury to the inner body. This is true; arms and legs of an inner body can indeed stretch to amazing lengths, perhaps 25 feet or longer. I have experienced this phenomenon, although not often. Why or how this stretching occurs I have yet to discover.

For example, one night I was out of body standing on a second-level balcony of what appeared to be an Earthlike apartment building. Somehow I fell backwards over the balcony railing. Keeping me calm about not suffering harm or pain was my good consciousness. Why my legs began to stretch I do not know, perhaps my lack of fear triggered this, but while falling backwards at a slow, safe speed my feet remained in place on the balcony floor. Calmly I watched as my inner-body legs elongated, stretching to about 20 feet in length and half diameter. When my back made soft contact with the ground below, my feet then lifted off the balcony floor and my legs slowly retracted to normal length and size. Lying face up on the ground, I felt no pain from the stretching or the fall and could only wonder about this oddity. Did my thoughts somehow induce the stretching, or was it an automatic reflex of some kind?

Occasionally my inner-body arms will stretch like this as well.

Telepathy: Part 2

Mental telepathy in the inner worlds I discussed in Chapter 4 of this book. But what about telepathy in the physical world? Is this possible?

I assume so. Some people reportedly have this gift. On

at least two occasions in recent years I may have experienced this myself. Once after reading about the afterlife, a silent message popped into my mind. Very clear and distinct, the message came in sentence form, one word after another, "You must learn how to teach." Another time after waking in the morning and reflecting upon a recent mistake I had made, a silent message passed through my mind, "Sometimes you have to take a step backward to progress spiritually." Both messages gave me the impression that something or someone had spoken to me silently. Perhaps I've received other mental messages and did not recognize them, or later forgot them.

Another kind of telepathy may also be possible. Some years ago while writing a letter to a friend of mine I intended to include a comment which suddenly slipped my mind. Try as I might, I could not remember the remark until after the letter was sealed in an envelope for mailing. Then my memory brought the comment back, but I decided against reopening the envelope. Good thing, because unbeknownst to me the letter would soon be opened and read by someone who should not have done so. Had my comment been included, there would have been big trouble for my friend. Did something or someone blank a thought from my mind somehow, or was it coincidence or luck? At the time, considering the possible consequences for my friend, I had to wonder and be thankful.

Calling For The Master

Finding the Inner Master in the nonphysical worlds is not a difficult trick. If I am out of body with enough consciousness to remember him, calling his name outloud may bring him. The Inner Master won't always make an appearance upon request, but the chances are reasonably good.

The same can be done by other soul-travelers and

dream-travelers as well because the Inner Master assists all Souls everywhere. For example, assume that you have contemplated in some manner and drifted into sleep. Suddenly you become conscious of either being out of body or leaving your body. If your consciousness is good enough to think about the Inner Master, you call outloud for him to appear. Several things can now occur. He may not show; you look around but nothing happens. Another possibility is that he appears before you. As if materializing out of nothing, the Master suddenly forms in front of you into a solid three-dimensional person, able to walk and talk. But more commonly if he shows he will do so discreetly. You look around and see him not far away, maybe opening a door.

All of these I have witnessed in the nonphysical planes, but without pomp is how the Master usually reveals himself to me. He may open a door and walk into a room where I happen to be at the time, or be standing behind me or a short distance away when I look around. He will act as if he has been present all along, and may walk over to converse with me.

My one concern about being with the Master in the inner worlds has already been mentioned. I have learned that when I am with him, especially if he is talking to me, I routinely begin hoping not to return to my physical self. Any such thoughts about my physical form will ordinarily send me back inside it. Because of this I do not often call for the Master during my OOBE's anymore. Knowing what will probably happen if he shows up, my preference is to remain out of body as long as I can.

Secrets

Not often, but a few times that I can remember, my hearing has somehow been tampered with in the inner planes. Once after I asked the Inner Master a question, he walked up to me and whispered words in my ear which sounded muffled. Another time a stranger answered a question of mine (I don't recall my question to him now) but for some reason his reply came out garbled, like a record player being slowed down. I asked this man the same question several more times and each of his replies sounded the same, garbled. My hearing otherwise during those OOBE's was fine; only select answers to certain questions that I asked were altered. Such temporary hearing problems while out of body I believe are caused by something or someone else. More than once I've grown angry realizing that I was not allowed to consciously hear and understand something said to me.

I also feel certain, however, that my temporary hearing losses in the inner planes are not ill-intended. Something or someone, maybe the Inner Master or Spirit, prevented me from hearing or understanding something for a reason. Presumably I'm not consciously ready for some information yet; this I can accept. Maybe someday.

Words And Voices

This morning it happened to me again. After waking early and making a trip to the bathroom, I hopped back into bed and slipped into sleep. Seeing pages of words on my inner mind screen was the next thing I became conscious of. Focusing on the wording to try and read and remember, suddenly the words changed from English to another written language that I did not recognize. I only picked up a few title words in English before the change.

Seeing words on my inner mind screen happens often in my sleep, either sentences, paragraphs, or full pages. Usually the words are typed or in graphics, as was the case today, rather than handwritten. If I gain enough consciousness to focus and read, however, the words will probably disappear or change. Apparently this printed information is meant more for my subconscious viewing than my conscious mind.

Hearing voices in my sleep also happens although not as frequently. Such voices can be male or female. Here again, though, if I gain enough consciousness to try and remember what is being said, the talking will likely cease. This phenomenon, too, seems intended for my subconscious learning.

Long Black Tunnel

Ever had an OOBE that simulated a long black tunnel? I had one during my first year of soul-traveling. One morning after waking I went back to sleep with my inner vision pointed at my inner mind screen. Suddenly I was conscious, in a solid body surrounded by blackness. Blowing against me was a gentle wind, maybe 10 miles per hour. Lying on my back, it felt like I was being sucked backwards through a long black tunnel as the wind tossed the hair on my inner-body head. This sensation lasted only a matter of seconds, though, before the darkness changed to a lighted environment with people present.

Publications about out-of-body travel and life after death commonly refer to a long black tunnel. Was my experience scary? My only concern was not knowing my destination. The rest was fun.

Breathing Underwater

Not long before I learned about soul travel, an uncle of mine told an interesting story to my family. As a youngster he and his brothers and father had gone to a swimming hole for a dip. Unable to swim then, my uncle inadvertently floated into a pool of water over his head when his father wasn't watching. Splashing about in desperation, gulping water and trying to breathe, he went under a third time before his father came to the rescue. What happened on that third plunge was the heart of the story. My uncle's eyes widened when he described having taken a deep breath underwater on his third descent. But how? He was certain of having been underwater when his chest expanded for that last full breath. Then he was dragged to safety.

I remembered this story after my soul-traveling began. How can a person take a breath underwater? What did my uncle really experience that day?

My early soul-traveling years brought several OOBE's whereby I was plunged beneath water, either voluntarily or not, in a nonphysical world. Several times when this occurred my consciousness was good enough for me to remember the story above. Curious about what had happened to my uncle, and also confident about not harming myself, I purposely tried breathing underwater. The water surrounding my inner body felt just like that on Earth. I opened my mouth, inhaled, but no water entered my mouth. Each time was the same: big breath, chest expansion, no water. Ordinarily while out of body I do not breathe, this I have learned, but I can make my inner-body chest expand and contract just like breathing. Doing this in the inner worlds, even underwater, feels the same as breathing here on Earth in my physical body.

Having experienced this, here is what I suspect may have happened to my uncle years ago when he nearly drowned. On that third plunge beneath the water's surface, because of his peril and panic, my uncle may have unknowingly shifted into one of his inner bodies while still inside his physical form. Like projecting out of body the moment before death or before an accident, he may have automatically taken sanctuary in an inner body. Desperately in need of air, he was suddenly able to inhale, or so it felt like. His chest expanded as if he had physically taken a breath of air, yet he was underwater. Afterward he vividly remembered having taken a big breath underwater, but how? If he was in one of his inner bodies at the time, this could be done. Otherwise, unless he inhaled water which felt like air, I can only wonder.

Strange Happening

Just days ago I became conscious during sleep of hanging onto the outside of something moving at high speed (afterward I wasn't sure what it was). For fun I decided to let go. Releasing my grip, I began to fall into a soft white sky that had no visible bottom. Fear I didn't feel because of my good consciousness. Immediately a solid invisible arm reached out from the sky and caught my inner body in a horizontal position. Realizing that the arm belonged to some protector, I said outloud, "Thank you, Spirit. Thank you, God. Thank you, (his name) Living Master."

Something strange then happened. Two arms reached downward through the top of my *physical head,* full length which I could feel, and shook my right inner-body hand one at a time. Remember, I was conscious in an inner body when this happened, lying horizontal on top of a solid arm, surrounded by a soft white sky. The two arms from above each shook my hand, then both pulled upward out of my *physical head.* Seconds later I was surrounded by my physical senses again.

Very interesting about this OOBE was my being able to feel the two arms push downward through my physical head while I was conscious in an inner body. Do nonphysical worlds exist within the area occupied by my physical body? This experience would suggest that answer to be yes. Can dream-traveling be done inside the physical form? Again this OOBE would suggest yes. Also, here is another example of nonphysical hands being able to penetrate the physical body to touch an inner body.

Positive-Thinking, Self Criticism, Meditation, Concentration, Contemplation

Prior to discovering soul travel I went through a self-discovery period. First it was positive-thinking which lasted about nine months.

My enthusiasm about applying positive-thinking to my everyday life did not endure, though; benefits were only short-term for me.

Then came several months of self-examination and self-criticism to try and better myself. Second-guessing my daily thoughts and actions as being good or bad eroded my confidence and happiness, however. After realizing this, I brought an end to daily self-analysis.

My next experiment was meditation. A couple of books on the subject sounded interesting so I decided to give it a try. Surprisingly, doing a meditative exercise each day for twenty minutes or so had a noticeably relaxing effect on me. For this reason I continued my daily meditations for about eight months until soul travel caught my fancy.

Concentration is how I achieved my early OOBE's. My odds of success were poor, though, and my ability to concentrate never did improve. To the contrary, the more concentration attempts that I mentally labored through, the poorer my ability to focus my thoughts. Eventually I quit trying.

Contemplation I learned by accident. After unexpectedly leaving my body one night in a state of total relaxation, my interest in contemplation soared. Unlike concentration which is an attempt to lock the mind perfectly onto an image or a feeling, contemplation is simply thinking about something in a relaxed manner. Whenever the mind wanders, which will happen often, the thought or feeling is brought back again. Contemplating like this until falling asleep is not easy, perhaps requiring a couple of hours or more, but doesn't strain the brain like concentration can.

Boxer

Several years ago I had two interesting OOBE's days apart. Finding myself out of body one night, standing in an inner world that looked similar to Earth, I first scanned my surroundings before noticing a subtle light pressure on both of my hips. Realizing that someone was standing behind me touching my hips, I made no move to indicate my awareness of that person's presence. Instead, feeling somewhat angered and insulted at this unseen individual for not giving me more space, I consciously and knowingly jabbed a quick right-hand punch over my left shoulder without turning my head. My aim was where I suspected that person's face to be.

To explain my aggressive behavior here, it is important to understand that emotions can be felt in some of the nonphysical worlds. The astral body is reportedly the source of emotions. Not infrequently my projections involve strong emotions and brash or reckless behavior which indicates an astral setting. During the OOBE mentioned above, my consciousness was very good but my feelings of dismay were strong also. If someone in this physical world crowds me close or holds onto me, I can feel this same ire. Angrily I struck a sharp blow over my left shoulder, hitting that person squarely in the face. Turning, I saw the Inner Master lying on the ground.

Unconcerned at this sight, I began running away, not for embarrassment or shame at my deed but to put distance between me and the person who'd been holding me. Obstacles of all sorts began appearing in front of me, obstructing my path and slowing me down. Jumping or crawling over, under, and around these magical barriers, it wasn't long before I lost control and shifted back inside my physical self. The next morning I chalked this up as another of my undisciplined astral journeys.

Several nights later came a sister OOBE. During sleep I found myself standing in a dream world, conscious of hands touching my hips from behind. Like before, feelings of anger flared up in me; that person was violating my space. Again I aimed a quick right-hand punch over my left shoulder. This time, however, my fist was slowed to a stop about halfway by an energy force. Then two hands reached around from behind me and grabbed both of my wrists, clasping them tightly against my chest. While struggling unsuccessfully to free myself, I automatically shifted back inside my physical form. The next morning I could only wonder if the person behind me had been the Inner Master.

Punching an Inner Master or anyone else for that matter is nothing to advertise, of course. But because strong emotions are sometimes felt in the lower nonphysical worlds, recklessness like this can occur there. Presumably the Inner Master is accustomed to dealing with unruly behavior, in the astral plane and elsewhere, and can take care of himself. Like a teacher waiting patiently for his students to mature, he watches them flounder and learn.

Most intriguing to me about this two-act drama was my boxing scorecard. When my first punch landed, I could only assume that the Inner Master had not known my punch was coming. He apparently didn't read my mind. But my second punch was anticipated and thwarted. That the Inner Master did not read my mind the first time and may have learned something about me through hard experience was fascinating to me. Could it be that the Inner Master did not know everything about me, such as my thoughts? Did my thoughts in the inner planes need to be spoken in silent sentences to be read telepathically? Was this true in the physical world as well?

Question Band

Author Paul Twitchell used a phrase "question band" to describe a period of time when beginning soul-travelers are filled with questions. Questions multiply without many answers to satisfy.

I can relate to this "question band" concept. My first two years of soul-traveling brought one question after another. What about this? Is such a thing possible? How about that? How to do this? Where did that happen and how? My questions were endless.

Eventually my "question period" passed. Gradually I became comfortable with knowing only a little about soul travel and related esoteric topics. Some answers I managed to learn, but most I did not know and stopped fretting about. If the answers came, fine. If not, fine. In the meantime, I was and still am going to have fun with my soul-traveling and dream-traveling, regardless.

Telekinesis

A dictionary defines telekinesis as the ability to mentally move an object without touching that object. Whether this is possible in the physical realm is debated. But in the inner worlds telekinesis is easy to do. Many times while out of body have I consciously moved nonphysical objects with my mind. To accomplish this I mentally concentrate on raising an object and usually move my inner-body arms in tandem with my thoughts. Like a magician levitating something from a distance, I extend my arms and imagine an object rising up. Distance does not matter; whether close or far I can still raise an object with my mind. Directional control I will have; I can mentally lift and move an object in any direction that my thoughts dictate. Size of an object does matter. The larger an object, the more difficult for me to mentally lift and move that object around. But a lapse in mental concentration will allow a levitated object to fall to the ground.

Having described this phenomenon, I should also add here that I may be receiving help when I perform this feat in the inner planes. My thoughts alone may not do the lifting. Something or someone else, maybe Spirit or the Inner Master, could be reading my arm movements and/or my thoughts and do the lifting on cue. But whatever the cause for telekinesis in the inner worlds, it is great fun to do and witness.

Silver Cord

Still puzzling to me is how the physical body is attached to its inner bodies. Metaphysical books speak of a silver cord which does this, but little about the silver cord do I understand.

Only once have I seen what may have been my silver cord. One morning after waking in the early hours and falling asleep again, I became partially conscious of who and where I was. Remembering about out-of-body travel, I sleepily lifted my inner body to a sitting position in bed. Able to see the interior of my sleeping room through the dim light, I took notice of a tube-like cord which dangled down across my chest from the back of my inner-body head. Coiling down around my inner-body feet on the floor, the cord glowed pale blue, perhaps a dozen feet of it being visible to me. Sleepily handling it, the cord felt like flexible plastic tubing, maybe a quarter inch in diameter. Out of curiosity I gave it a gentle tug which caused a mild pain where the cord attached to my inner-body head. Consciously realizing that this might be my silver cord, I refrained from pulling on it for fear of causing damage to the cord or to me. An automatic return to my physical form came while holding this thin blue tube.

During no other OOBE have I ever detected a cord attached to my inner body. Numerous times while separated from my physical self I have looked and felt with my hands all around my inner body, searching for a cord, but none was there. Even while flying I have reached around me in all directions but no umbilical cord, only hands of a person flying behind me holding onto my feet.

Although I assume that some kind of cord does link my physical body to my different inner bodies, it isn't clear to me how. Writings describe the silver cord as being visible and touchable from the physical body to the astral body, or at least sometimes visible and touchable from the physical body to the astral body. Connecting the astral body to the causal body to the mental body, the silver cord is apparently not visible and not touchable. This cord is also said to have stretch capabilities. When physical death comes, the silver cord is somehow severed permanently from the deceased physical body.

Questions I could ask about the silver cord abound. Is the silver cord sometimes detectable and sometimes not? If so, why and how? What is the silver cord made of, solid substance or not? How can an invisible, undetectable cord connect inner bodies together? Is the silver cord attached to the Soul body? Does the silver cord stretch, and if so, how? Do thoughts and information flow from one inner body to another or to the physical brain via the silver cord? How is the silver cord severed at death? Answers to questions like these would be helpful.

Auras

Although I know individuals who claim to see auras around people sometimes, I cannot recall ever seeing a colored glow around anyone. What little I know about auras comes from reading. I am convinced, though, that each person (Soul) and perhaps every living thing is surrounded by a colored aura.

A brother of mine surprised me with an interesting aura story during my first months of soul-traveling. I was giving him an enthusiastic spiel about out-of-body travel when he interrupted my monologue to announce that a colored aura had become visible around me. I looked and could see nothing, but he was certain of seeing two colors, green tinged with red, surrounding me. These colors remained visible to him for some time, several minutes anyway, before dissipating.

Books say that the color of a person's aura can reveal much about that person's personality, health, and spiritual progress. For this reason spiritually advanced individuals can know much about a person at a glance, if an aura is visible. Change in a person's personality, health, and/or spiritual consciousness will change the color of that person's aura.

Blue Man

One night a mystery man appeared in my bedroom. After waking in the night and falling asleep again contemplating, I suddenly felt myself jerk upward a short distance. Finding myself fully conscious and wide awake, suspended horizontally on my back in an inner body above my physical form, through dim light I could see the inside of my sleeping room. In front of me I could also see a blue human shape from the waist up. The bottom half of this blue three-dimensional transparency I could not see, but the legs were solid. Bent in a mid-air sitting position, the legs of this blue visitor were pressed against my right inner-body thigh.

To avoid causing an automatic return to my physical self I remained motionless. Having full consciousness kept me relatively calm, in spite of the ghostly blue face staring at me, eyes visible only as fuzzy holes. Feeling somewhat apprehensive about being with this stranger, I decided to show friendship by reaching out my right inner-body arm and placing my hand on the blue person's forearm. The blue person then did the same, reaching out and placing his/her hand on my right inner-body arm. Gaining confidence, I took the friendly lead again and asked in a voice which sounded like my physical voice, "Is your name Sufi?" This name I had picked up in a prior dream. From the blue face came a verbal reply, "Yes." Encouraged by this response, I next asked, "Are you male or female?", to which the reply was male. I followed with another question, "How old are you?" The answer was twenty-one. Wondering why this blue man was with me, I asked, "Do you want to come back to the physical world?", which brought another short response, "Yes." Still lying motionless with my hand resting on the blue-man's forearm and his on mine, trying to keep my fears and emotions in check as best as possible, my next remark was, "I thought the inner worlds were supposed to be much more beautiful than the physical world." For the first time the blue-man's response was more than a single word. Speaking verbally for maybe ten seconds, he made a statement that each person's world is created within that person, which sounded wise but seemed to contradict his notion of wanting to return to the physical plane.

My excitement began to escalate here which suddenly moved me downward into my physical form. Lying motionless with good recall of this surprise encounter, still noticeable was the faint touch of the blue-man's leg and hand on my inner body. By remaining still and falling asleep again I would have shifted out of body automatically into the presence of this same blue man; this I knew. But seeing him again did not appeal to me so I rolled over to a more comfortable position in bed and went back to sleep. Moving my physical body broke the contact between my inner body and the blue man's. He didn't revisit me that night, nor has he since.

Believing Or Knowing

The difference between believing and knowing something is simply this: A person who believes doesn't yet know for certain.

There are people who believe that out-of-body travel is possible, and there are those who believe that out-of-body travel is not possible. People who know have consciously experienced this phenomenon.

There are people who believe that nonphysical worlds exist, and there are those who believe that nonphysical worlds do not exist. People who know have consciously visited the inner planes in a solid inner body.

Nobody knows that inner worlds do not exist nor that out-of-body travel is not possible. People who say no to either of these are merely voicing opinions.

This brings to mind a story dating back some years when I paid a visit to some Catholic friends of mine. The family priest happened by while I was there and one of the boys in the family told the priest that I and other people could project out of body. The priest quietly but sternly told the boy that such a thing is not possible, which didn't convince the boy.

Spiritual Eye

Closing the eyes and looking at the upper base of the nose will target one of several soul-travel windows within the physical body. The blackness there, called the Spiritual Eye, is evidently opened and closed by the pineal gland inside the head.

Sometimes during contemplation or after returning from an OOBE I will become conscious of a picture on my inner mind screen. The picture may be large, covering the entire black inner screen, or visible through a small circular hole in the blackness. Focusing my inner vision on such a scene can send me into that inner-world setting. If this happens, the two-dimensional picture becomes three-dimensional when I join it.

Another possibility can also occur if the Spiritual Eye opens. I may be able to see physical objects in my bedroom through my forehead (with my eyelids closed). The Spiritual Eye is delicate, though, and will usually turn black if any part of the physical body is moved.

Sounds Of The Planes

Each world that has life, nonphysical and physical, has a sound associated with it which reverberates from Spirit. The roar of the sea, tinkling bells, buzzing of bees, single note of a flute, heavy wind, and deep humming are sounds I have heard during my contemplations or inner travels. Such tones can indicate which plane a person is experiencing. Only a high whistle do I hear often, however, which sounds like a single note of a flute inside my head. All of my contemplations as well as some of my waking hours bring this faint high whistle which comes and goes intermittently inside my head.

Heavy wind I have felt while out of body, usually while flying. Being buffeted by a strong wind in the inner planes has never harmed me, though.

The sound of the physical plane is thunder. This could be what I hear now and then as a loud bang inside my head while contemplating or during sleep.

Deep humming I have heard more than once while softly chanting myself to sleep repeating HU. Emanating from inside my head, the humming had a soothing, supernatural quality to it. I could only wonder how it was happening.

Buzzing I've heard several times while contemplating

or asleep which brings to mind a funny story. One morning while trying to snooze with a bedsheet over my head a buzzing started near my right ear. Angrily I raised my hand and swatted a couple of times, assuming a fly to be nearby. Relaxing under the covers again, the buzzing came back minutes later so again I shook the bedcover and waved my hand about. This same pattern repeated a couple of more times before I finally jumped out of bed to get a flyswatter. When I couldn't find a fly anywhere is when I began to wonder about the buzzing.

Foot Massage

One night after returning from an OOBE I went back to sleep softly repeating the name of the Living Master. Suddenly I was conscious in the midst of blackness, seemingly without a body form which was odd. Then beside me appeared a rectangular color picture of the Living Master sitting in a chair, showing body movement. A voice came from the darkness which I assumed was the Master's, professing a great love for me. My growing excitement hearing and seeing this caused a shift back inside my physical form.

Lying in bed reflecting on what had just transpired, I was about to begin contemplating again when my feet distracted me. It took a moment for me to realize that two hands were gently rubbing my feet and ankles as if to relax and soothe me, first one foot and then the other, back and forth. Hardly believing this was happening, I lay motionless, trying my best to enjoy this foot massage. How was this possible? Because my inner body was still my dominant body is why my inner-body feet (inside my physical feet) could still be touched by nonphysical hands. Unfortunately, my growing excitement gradually awakened my physical body. As my physical senses slowly returned, the touch of the hands rubbing my inner-body feet gradually faded away.

The Armpit Story

My early soul-travel adventures saw the beginnings of an interesting drama. During some of my inner travels I was grabbed from behind and held, in most cases when my behavior was reckless or belligerent. Oftentimes when this happened I was unaware of anyone even being in back of me. Hands would suddenly reach around from behind me and pin my arms against my chest, apparently to stop my misconduct. Sometimes I managed to get a look at the person behind me and sometimes not if the commotion caused an automatic return to my physical self. The person responsible usually turned out to be a stranger rather than the Inner Master.

Then came an OOBE where somebody grabbed me from behind by my armpits instead of my arms. This caused a tickling in my armpits which immediately put me back inside my physical form. After this, a pattern developed. As if people in the inner planes had learned about my ticklish armpits, my OOBE's involving reckless or belligerent behavior frequently ended with me being grabbed from behind by my armpits.

Eventually I learned about fly-behind people and other helping companions in the inner worlds. Most of them were strangers to me but I learned not to fear these people; they were not the enemy or malintentioned. Always it irked me, though, whenever I was grabbed from behind by my armpits to end an OOBE. This I did not like because of wanting to remain out of body as long as possible.

For years this scenario repeated until one night when I returned from the nonphysical planes for this same reason. Lying motionless in bed, fuming mad, I remembered about mental telepathy. Wanting to vent my anger to anyone capable of listening, I began speaking silent words and sentences in my mind. The gist of my demands was this: I did not want anyone or anything to ever again grab me by my armpits during any of my future OOBE's. My words didn't mince my wrath.

Since then I have been grabbed from behind by my armpits only once while out of body. That one instance was by a middle-aged lady unfamiliar to me. After she grabbed me, my consciousness was good enough for me to quickly turn around and force her hands from my armpits. Angrily I gave her a tongue-lashing before my temper put me back inside my physical form.

There are still times when I am grabbed from behind and held by my wrists or arms during my OOBE's. Usually when this happens I'm behaving recklessly or belligerently or worse, perhaps because of poor consciousness. But the word about my armpits is apparently out--no more armpit-grabbing. I will be surprised if this happens to me again in the future.

Helpful Hints

Over the years I have learned of two hindrances to projecting out of body.

First, in the middle of the night it is common for me to feel bladder pressure. If I ignore this discomfort and do not get up out of bed for bladder relief, my chances of a conscious projection out of body that night are poor. Whether I contemplate or not, bladder pressure will sharply reduce my chances for a conscious OOBE. Getting out of bed in the night or early morning for a restroom call not only eliminates the physical distraction of bladder pressure, my conscious mind is also awakened for contemplation which greatly improves my OOBE chances.

A second hindrance is body temperature. Being too hot or too cold can make soul travel or dream travel difficult. An electric blanket putting out too much heat, or a room too cold, can cause enough physical discomfort to prevent or reduce the chances for conscious out-of-body travel.

Flying Improves OOB Consciousness

Even as a beginning soul-traveler I recognized that flying in the inner worlds could improve my conscious thinking capability. Because my consciousness in the inner planes can vary anywhere from none to excellent, quite often while out of body I will realize that my conscious awareness is not 100%. When this happens, I may remember that flying can improve my consciousness. By mentally raising myself up off the ground, either levitating my inner body or flying, I will usually be able to think more conscious thoughts than before. Why this is I have not figured out, though.

Drugs

People have asked me if I use drugs to induce my OOBE's. The answer is no. Drugs, alcohol, and cigarettes I can do without. All are detrimental to physical health as well as spiritual health.

Whether drug-induced "trips" that other people experience and report are visits into the inner planes or controllable or conscious, I cannot say.

Love And Ego

Religious and spiritual leaders universally emphasize love as a bridge to spiritual enlightenment and the heavens. Something I have noticed in people is that the more love a person feels about anything, a mate, family, life, job, religion, the Inner Master, God, whatever, the less ego that person is likely to show. But the more ego a person displays, the less love that person feels. Ego seems to displace love.

Letter To The Newspaper Editor

Something wonderful happened to me the other day. A little girl looked up into my eyes and said hi.

It was unexpected. I was walking along the city sidewalks thinking only of tasks to do that day. Approaching a street corner, there she was, a small girl in a wheelchair being pushed by her mother. I glanced only briefly at her, bent on other projects for the day, but her eyes caught mine in that moment and wouldn't let go of me.

Straps held her upright in her wheelchair, straps across her chest, stomach, and shoulders, and still she could not hold herself up straight. Her head drooped down to one side. But in her eyes and "hi" there was only joy. For a couple of seconds I couldn't divert my eyes from hers which radiated so much happiness. Life's difficulties she did not yet understand. All she cared about was being alive now.

It happened so quickly that I was past her within seconds, and yet those eyes and that friendly "hi" I could still see and hear as I walked on down the street. Half an hour later it happened again. Turning another street corner, there she was again, the small girl being wheeled ahead of her mother. This time I noticed her first and stopped to say hi, taking her tiny hand in mine which she raised with difficulty. A miracle healing is what I wanted for her although I knew such ailments carry spiritual purpose.

Later I thought about how nice it would be if all people in this city and elsewhere could look into this little girl's eyes and see the joy there. Surely their troubles wouldn't seem so heavy.

signed Terrill Willson
address and phone

Raindrops

Recently I experienced something new in the inner planes--raindrops.

During a dream I became conscious enough to realize that I was already out of body, high in a sky riding a roller coaster. Up and down and around curves the roller coaster went, through light skies and dark, with me and other passengers aboard laughing and having great fun. On one occasion when our roller coaster plowed into a darkened sky that felt noticeably cool and moist, a shower of water drops came pelting down. Just like a rain shower here on Earth is what it felt like. But after passing through this brief rain shower, it was odd that the water droplets left no signs of wetness. All passengers and clothing were perfectly dry as we continued our merry meandering roller-coaster ride through the sky.

Auto-Oxidation

Some years ago I watched a television newscast about an elderly doctor found dead inside his home, charred to ashes. Wisps of blue smoke still lingered in the air when a visitor discovered the doctor's remains. Not all of the clothing on the body was burned, however, and minimal damage showed inside the room. Reduced to ashes were the body and much of the clothing, but little else.

The news reporter then turned his interview to a researcher who had long studied this strange phenomenon of spontaneous human incineration, called auto-oxidation. The researcher had compiled dozens of documented cases like the one described above. A person is suddenly cremated, sometimes without the clothing on the body being burned. How is this possible? Ordinary cremation of a deceased physical body requires heat and fire of more than a thousand degrees temperature. How can a body be reduced to ashes indoors without burning the building or damaging the structure?

At the time of watching this news story I was familiar with soul travel. To me the mystery of auto-oxidation was no mystery at all. I could picture it in my mind. When the time for death came, Spirit detached the elderly doctor from his physical body and then, for whatever reason, incinerated that body to ashes. Probably there was no pain at all for the doctor who may have even stood by and watched the cremation of his flesh and bones. Then the doctor was transported in his inner body to some nonphysical plane for a stay there. Earth people gazed upon the charred remains of the doctor with horror and wonder. How terrible! Someone please explain this!

Recorded cases of auto-oxidation stretch the imagination even further. People still alive who are nowhere near fire, sometimes in cold climate, have suddenly caught fire and begun to burn with a blue flame. Usually such incidents result in death, although not always. Clothing on the body may even go undamaged which deepens the mystery.

That people are baffled by auto-oxidation is understandable. Any explanation has to point to Spirit rather than science. Why Spirit would incinerate a body or set a person aflame remains a question. But the how is not difficult to visualize. Spirit has intelligence and can funnel Its energy through anything at any time. Like a zap from a ray gun, Spirit could reduce a physical body or anything else to ashes instantly. Its power is beyond human comprehension. Science will forever puzzle over the riddle of auto-oxidation because the answer lies with Spirit.

Demons

What are demons? People talk about evil spirits and demons. Religions harp on this subject. Yet as many times as I've consciously been out of body, I don't know what a demon is.   Strange-looking creatures and people I have seen from time to time in the inner worlds, some of them aggressive, but were they demons? Not likely. Never have any of them harmed me.

Not long ago I met a talkative fellow (here on Earth) who took it upon himself to educate me about religious history, Christianity, and the Bible. Trying to impress and win me over to his viewpoints, he finally asked me what I thought about demons. Realizing that he would soon be lecturing me about demons, I surprised him. I told him that I had consciously been out of body many times in the nonphysical worlds and had not seen any demons. Creatures and ugly people I'd seen there, but I didn't know what a demon was. Would he please tell me? His oration came to an abrupt halt. He couldn't think of anything else to say.

I still don't know.   Sometimes I hear people, particularly preachers or religious ardents, talk about demons this and demons that. Watch out for them because they are bad and they may get you, somehow, somewhere. I must say that if there is one thing I am not concerned about, it is demons. I cannot imagine how one or more of them could harm me, if they exist and if they wanted or tried to.

Ghosts

Are ghosts for real? Documented ghost sightings are so numerous that I have to believe so. My assumption is that ghosts are either deceased people/animals from this physical life, or else astral entities that become temporarily visible to human eyes. It is said that strong emotional attachment to places or people on Earth can hold an astral body in the physical arena for some time after physical death. This seems plausible, at least to me.

Two ghost stories that I know of could be true. Days

after a mother died, she appeared in her daughter's bedroom. The adult daughter told me that her deceased mother, looking human, lay on her (the daughter's) bed and carried on a verbal conversation with her. When the conversation ended, the mother disappeared and left behind a body imprint that remained on the bed for several days. Another story comes from a television show that I watched years ago. Video news investigation of a haunted retail store was undertaken. A psychic brought to the store was able to communicate with a ghost there by speaking verbally and receiving telepathic replies. She pointed to where the ghost was standing, described him as a young man, and learned his name, age, and other details about him. A video tape of that area in the store revealed no ghost--except for one video frame. A single frame in the video captured a sharp color picture of a young man leaning against an isle display rack near the psychic. The young man's appearance matched the psychic's description of him.

What these and other ghost stories tell me is that ghosts probably do exist here on Earth, for reasons of attachment or something else. Sightings account for most of the ghost lore although communication between ghosts and Earth people is sometimes reported.

Should ghosts be feared? Perhaps a better question to ask is why are ghosts feared? Astral or spiritual beings vibrate with greater energy than do physical objects and therefore cannot touch physical objects or people. Exceptions to this would be rare. So how can a ghost harm anyone? The widespread fear of ghosts evidently stems from fear of the unknown or things nonphysical.

Astral Sex

Can a person feel emotions like lust in the inner planes? Definitely yes. Oftentimes I am swayed by emotions while out of body: anger, lust, fear, excitement are all common for me. The astral body rather than the physical body is said to be the source of emotions. Whether emotions can be felt in the causal, mental, and Soul bodies I'm not sure, however.

Sometimes I feel lust so strongly while out of body that I become excessively forceful with (astral) women. Female companionship is not hard to find in the inner planes, and sexual advances are often permitted or tolerated by women there. Many times have I gotten involved in OOB kissing and hand-groping sessions over the years. Such foreplay encounters can generate the same sexual excitement as here on Earth because the body contact, kisses, and tastes are just as real. A male inner body can indeed acquire a penis erection, this I've learned, but never have I been able to perform sexual intercourse with a female in the nonphysical planes. Always my overexcitement has caused an automatic shift back inside my physical self.

If I was to guess about sexual intercourse being possible in the inner (astral) worlds, however, my guess would be yes.

Astral Sex Continued

My first writing of Astral Sex (above) turned out too descriptive and long, detailing sexual foreplay and attempted intercourse in my inner body. Upon review I decided to summarize for a wider audience.

The night that I rewrote Astral Sex, I lay down at bedtime and did a short repetition of HU before going to sleep. Much of that night I spent in lucid dreams until one of my dreams turned into a conscious OOBE. I became aware of a pair of hands and an upper body gently hugging and caressing my inner-body head. Realizing that I was already out of body, I kept my eyes closed and carefully raised my inner-body arm to touch a female. For maybe fifteen seconds I enjoyed her caresses on my face until suddenly the blackness in front of my closed eyes changed to a picture of a house. Startled by this, my inner-body eyelids popped open to discover a dimly lighted three-dimensional house maybe 50 feet in front of me, the same white and green house in the picture. Everything else around me remained black.

Seeing the house sent a cold chill through me because a past-life story flashed through my mind. The girl slid down behind me and started sobbing, wrapping her arms around my chest as if in fear. At some time in my past, in some other life, I had sexually assaulted this female inside a house that looked like this one. I was now being given an opportunity to review something bad from my past, to help put that deed to rest and burn off karma.

What kept me in control of my emotions and fears here was my full consciousness. Confident that this was a learning opportunity and not punishment, I reached back and took hold of an arm of the sobbing woman whom I could not yet see, then moved slowly toward the house. I don't recall now whether I walked or mentally floated myself forward through the darkness. But while moving I spoke to the lady in back of me, verbally reassuring her that everything would be okay. Reaching the front door, I opened it and cautiously stepped inside, still pulling on the crying female. Glancing around through a soft light, the room was small, much of it empty except for a sofa and bed. Turning my head, the lady emerged from blackness with hands raised to her face, trembling. Maybe 25-30 years of age, short with dark hair, clothed in a full-length white nightgown, she was overweight and unattractive. Obviously afraid, she followed reluctantly as I pulled her inside the room, telling her that she would not be harmed. Leading her to the bed where she lay down, still crying, her nightgown fluttered in a soft breeze that played about the room. Sitting down beside her, I could feel the past. This place, or a place like it, was where a cruel rape or sexual assault had once been committed by me against her. But this time I felt no such lust, only sympathy and understanding. Touching her face and shoulders, I tried calming her by explaining that we were both revisiting a place from the past, to soften painful memories from that time. Her fear and trembling began to subside. A weak smile crossed her face as she started to relax, reaching out one of her hands to touch me.

Then suddenly a wooden sculpture appeared not far behind the prone lady's head, visible to me but not to her. Showing a man's face and shoulders, it looked like a totem pole about three feet tall. Realizing that the carved face would surely frighten this woman if she saw it, I kept my attention on her and only glanced at the carving from time to time so she would not look back. Movement came to the eyes and facial expression on the totem image, showing life, yet my good consciousness kept me calm. Did the carving have something to do with the sexual crime I had once committed against this lady? Dark-haired, mustached, and Anglo, the face may have been my father's then. I didn't know, but this was my guess.

Then everything vanished. In an instant I was back inside my physical body again, surrounded by my physical senses. The lady's appearance and the carved image I could still visualize. I began to wonder: Could the wooden face have been mine in that former life?

Temporary Paralysis

While concentrating at bedtime years ago I slipped into sleep and became conscious of moving into blackness. Shortly after this, while descending into a lighted Earthlike world, there came a loud bang just outside the room where my physical body lay sleeping. Although conscious in an inner body, I clearly heard this noise and believed that someone was opening the door to where my physical body lay. Afraid that someone might see my physical self without me in it, I wanted desperately to return to my body that moment and raise up in bed. I could not make my physical body move, however. First I found myself being propelled headlong through darkness on my back for several seconds before my physical senses returned. Then I was able to jerk my body upright in bed, my heart racing in panic. Quickly I realized that the loud noise had been caused by a falling object outside my bedroom.

Not long ago while dream-traveling in the early morning, my alarm clock rang. Hearing the alarm and realizing what the noise was, I wanted and tried to shut the alarm off immediately. My physical body would not move, however. First I was drawn over a lighted inner world for a brief interval until my physical senses came back. Then I was able to reach over and shut off the alarm.

Other similar instances of temporary physical paralysis have happened to me while out of body, although not often. None have caused me any pain I might add. More likely if I am dream-traveling and hear a noise near my physical body, an automatic return to my physical self will occur instantly. This gives me immediate movement of my physical limbs.

Healing

I feel certain that Spirit can heal physical ailments. If Spirit is indeed the energy of God, then It should be able to do or alter anything in any world at any time.

There have been times when I have projected out of body and experienced a physical healing from an illness. This doesn't always happen, of course. I've been sick and left my body and received no healing. But from time to time I feel healing effects after an OOBE. Paranormal healings of mine have only been for minor ailments, though, like head congestion, fatigue, eye infection, etc.

Here are some general observations that I have made over the years about paranormal healings. Thus far my best healing success has been for glandular or sinus ailments inside my physical head. Apparently soul travel or dream travel can sometimes bring balance to glandular disorders, perhaps because of the pituitary or pineal glands being activated. Other illnesses like the flu, pneumonia, viruses, I've not had much luck with healing while out of body. Time is another factor. The longer I remain out of body, the better my chances for a healing. A brief projection may not allow enough time for any improvement in my physical condition. Consciousness can also play a role. I cannot recall ever receiving a paranormal healing without having good OOB consciousness. Lucid dreams and OOBE's with poor consciousness don't seem to affect my physical health.

Can Spirit cure any illness? My assumption is yes. More than once a strong current of energy has funneled through my physical body which gave me the feeling that Spirit can cure virtually anything. Wanting or asking for Spirit to cure a physical ailment is another matter, however. To my understanding Spirit has intelligence and a will of Its own. Prayers, willpower, pleadings from people for healings are not likely to persuade Spirit to intervene. Exceptions do happen, though.

Padre Pio

Curiosity had me reading about Padre Pio awhile back. Numerous books have been written about this revered Catholic priest who lived in Italy until his death in 1968. Paul Twitchell's writings tell of the padre and his reported bilocation capabilities which is how I learned of him. Much out of the ordinary was attributed to Padre Pio including bilocation, miracles, perfume smell, psychic abilities, spiritual enlightenment, even bleeding circles on his hands.

For about a week my thoughts dwelled on the padre. Then came a strange night. While asleep I became conscious enough to realize who and where I was. Soul travel came to mind so I tried crawling out of my physical body. I was sleepily pushing my inner-body arms and legs forward when two giant-sized hands, each maybe six feet in length, clasped my inner-body arms and gently pulled me into blackness. Palms together, the huge hands felt solid yet I could see through them.

The hands pulled me a short ways through darkness and then released me in front of a lighted wooden cross which was standing upright, maybe five feet tall. Attached to the cross was a large golden statue of a man with his arms outstretched. Fully conscious and now wide awake, my guess was that the giant transparent hands somehow belonged to Padre Pio and the gold figurine represented Jesus' crucifixion. I also realized, however, that the huge hands might be those of something or someone else, maybe the Inner Master, Jesus, Spirit, or some other Master. But my feeling was Padre Pio.

Here my mental and emotional control wavered, though. Backwards I began to gravitate through darkness, presumably toward my physical self. Then came the giant hands again, sandwiching my inner-body arms in between and pulling me back to a kneeling position in front of the cross and statue. When the hands let go of me, I bowed down before the golden statue and said outloud, "I respect your religion and your teacher", speaking as if to Padre Pio. "But I have a teacher of my own. His name is (the Living Master)." Before finishing the Master's name, however, my excitement at what was happening sent me backwards through darkness into my physical body.

Lucid dreams kept me entertained for the remainder of the night. The huge hands didn't perform again. Next morning I could only speculate about the cross, statue, and colossal hands. Was it a test of my devotion? By whom, Padre Pio? The Inner Master maybe?

Chapter 8

DEATH, PAST LIVES, KARMA

One conscious OOBE can change anyone's view of death. But afterward, will the fear of death be gone? Likely not. As many times as I have consciously left my body, I still fear death. Why? Because of instinct, a will to live. The human brain has a natural desire for life and an instinctive rejection of death. For most people, knowledge that life continues after death won't extinguish the fear of death. However, soul travel and conscious dream travel can reduce the fear of dying which is what I now feel. Since my soul-traveling began, my fear of death has diminished noticeably.

What about a loved one dying? Will a soul-traveler feel sorrow when a family member, relative, or friend dies? Should a soul-traveler feel sorrow? Family history has taught me that losing a loved one will still bring heartache and pain. Knowing that life does not end at death is comforting, but tears will still come.

Because all of us face death, the next question is: What happens afterward? What is the afterlife like? What do we consist of and what kind of world will we end up in? How long do we stay there? Forever?

From reading I have done, it is my understanding that relatively few individuals will be spiritually advanced enough at death to gain entry into God's eternal heavens, the Soul plane and above. For these enlightened Souls, this means a permanent return to the higher nonphysical worlds. Do solid or visible objects exist in the higher inner worlds, and is Soul bodiless or visible there? This I cannot say with certainty, unfortunately, because my OOBE's into the upper planes are probably few or none. Stories and descriptions that I have heard and read differ.

But physical death for all other people, which is most people, means either going to one of the lower inner planes (astral, causal, or mental) for a designated length of time, or immediately reincarnating into the physical world. The karma of each deceased individual is reviewed at the time of death by a Lord of Karma. Everything in that person's past is weighed in balance. Past lives and afterlives of the deceased are included in this summation, all of which are recorded in pictures. How hangs the balance, toward the good or bad? A Lord of Karma makes a decision, without error or argument. A deserving destination, good or bad, is selected. If immediate reincarnation into the physical world is the verdict, that individual, as Soul, reincarnates into another physical body with a new conscious mind. A subconscious mind retains information and knowledge from the past. If the astral, causal, or mental plane is chosen for the deceased person, he or she goes there for a specified time in a solid, visible inner body. The appearance of the inner body will apparently match that of the expired physical body but retain a youthful look. The nonphysical world will be solid to the touch and may or may not resemble Earth. After spending a certain amount of time there, that Soul will then reincarnate again into the physical world in a new physical body with another conscious mind.

Chapter 9

HELL AND HEAVEN

To date I've not seen a lake of fire in the lower nonphysical planes although I have no doubt that such firey places exist there. Do people on Earth who don't believe in a religious savior, or those carrying bad karma, burn in such lakes of fire after they die? Must bad people or nonbelievers forever endure a torturous Hell of some kind after death? Modern and ancient religions say no to both questions. Even the worst offenders endure an inner Hell of some kind for only so long before reincarnating again into the physical world.

Have I seen bad places in the inner worlds that reminded me of Hell? Yes, but not often. For example, one Earthlike environment had a gaseous atmosphere where people were laboring with gas masks on. Another dark place had deformed people huddled in groups like lepers. Never have I been harmed in such hideous places, though.

Seeing beauty in the inner planes is much more common for me, thankfully. The true eternal heavens of the Soul plane and above I am not sure I've ever visited. But heavens in the lower worlds I have witnessed often. What are they like and where are they? All of the lower nonphysical planes have them, countless places of splendor. Many such heavens have little or no resemblance to Earth. Colors, objects, terrain, and other things in non-Earthlike worlds can be wondrous.

Do people enjoy the bliss and beauty of astral, causal, and mental-plane heavens forever after they die? Evidently not; only for a span of time designated by a Lord of Karma. Then comes time for another reincarnation into the physical world as the cycle of birth and death continues.

Chapter 10

WHY REINCARNATION?

Reincarnation is becoming more widely recognized as part of God's plan to help each Soul acquire spiritual knowledge, experience, and wisdom. When a Soul acquires sufficient spiritual enlightenment in the lower planes, the reward is a permanent return to the higher eternal heavens after death of the physical body. How many reincarnations in the physical and lower worlds will a Soul need to reach this goal? Maybe thousands. Eons of time can elapse. For each Soul this will vary.

So how is spiritual progress measured? Both good and bad actions and thoughts in any of God's worlds result in learning. Good is preferred, of course. But spiritual advancement is evidently weighed more heavily by an enhanced understanding of what God's gameplan is all about. For individuals who begin to learn about God, Spirit, inner worlds, Godmen and the Inner Master, spiritual laws, self discipline, love, reincarnation and the cycle of birth and death, bilocation, heaven and Hell, etc., these are the Souls who begin to take spiritual strides.

How much spiritual progress is needed to end the cycle of reincarnations? No religion can claim the only path to God. It is possible for anyone to gain enough spiritual enlightenment in a lifetime to break the cycle of birth and death. But few will because the task is difficult, more difficult than people realize. A more practical way is finding and establishing ties with an authentic Godman so that when death comes, the Lord of Karma is bypassed. A protective Godman takes custody of a disciple after death rather than a Lord of Karma. If more spiritual growth is needed for that Soul to earn the permanent heavens, which is common, the Godman then escorts that Soul to one of the lower nonphysical planes for more time and learning there. Without directing or interfering in a person's life, a genuine Godman can continue to monitor and assist a Soul spiritually until the upper heavens are again rewon.

For every Soul, each lifetime in the physical world brings this same opportunity. Will Soul continue to struggle on the reincarnation treadmill, or discover and follow a true Godman who knows the path and pitfalls back to God's eternal heavens?

Chapter 11

CAUSE AND EFFECT

Spiritual laws of God are discussed in churches and households around the globe. The Law of Cause and Effect is an example, heard in familiar phrases: reap what you sow, do unto others as you would have them do unto you, things that you do and say in life will return to you, good karma brings heaven and bad karma brings Hell, love thy neighbor, etc. Interpretation of the Law of Cause and Effect is consistent, with one exception. Religions which reject the concept of reincarnation say that what a person sows in a physical life will someday be reaped again, either before or after a person's death. Religions which embrace reincarnation say that what a person sows in a physical life will someday be reaped again, either during the present life, an afterlife, or a future reincarnation. Perfect balance is another way to explain this principle. Every word and action is recorded and will eventually be balanced out, either during a person's present life, an afterlife, or a future reincarnation. So perfectly does this Law of Cause and Effect apparently unfold that Souls affecting the lives of other Souls will meet again in future lives, so karmic debts can be repaid.

Can a Soul's karma be lifted by a qualified savior, saint, or spiritual master? To my understanding a bonafide Godman can accept any share of any person's (Soul's) karma at any time. Seldom will this happen, however, because a Godman's role is teacher and guide rather than a basket for the sins of others. Accepting the karma of others would require the Godman himself to repay those karmic debts. Instead of doing this, a Godman helps disciples dissolve their own karmic burdens through dreams, OOBE's, and other means. This allows Souls to review and learn from their own doings, either consciously or subconsciously. To gain the assistance of a teaching Godman, asking is the first step, from within or direct. Capable Godmen, both physical and nonphysical, generally don't mingle in the affairs of others unless requested.

Can karma be avoided, in particular bad karma? It is said that every word and action creates good, bad, or neutral karma unless offered in the name of God. Words or deeds performed with God in mind create no karma and therefore reap no karmic effects in the future. Both good and bad karma eventually bring payment in kind; nothing is forgotten. In this way Soul learns and matures spiritually in the lower planes, through trial and error, experience, and sometimes with the aid of teachers.

Looking back at my own past, I can see much interweaving of cause and effect. Malice that I have done or shown toward others has later returned to me in strikingly similar fashion. Coincidences that occur in my life involving people or events make me wonder about past karmic debts or credits. Many of my presentday family, relatives, and friends were no doubt associated with me in previous lives. A Law of Cause and Effect that fits life together this perfectly warrants attention.

The same is evidently true for all levels of spiritual attainment. Each Soul progresses spiritually in the lower worlds until enough spiritual advancement is gained to deserve reentry into the higher inner heavens. Thereafter the learning process continues for each enlightened Soul because spiritual perfection is an impossibility except for God. Always there will be something new for Soul to do and learn, another spiritual step to take. Souls which develop the habit of thinking, speaking, and acting in the name of God create no karma and therefore bypass the Law of Cause and Effect. But when any Soul, enlightened or otherwise, fails to act, think, or speak in God's name, karma is then created. In other words, no Soul, regardless of how spiritually elevated, is above the Law of Cause and Effect. Actions, thoughts, and words manifested without God in mind will create good, bad, or neutral karma which in turn sets in motion cause and effect.

Consider a Soul spiritually ready for the upper heavens. Continued learning and spiritual unfoldment for that Soul will bring a stronger flow of Spirit along with enhanced Godlike capabilities. But the drawback to this accomplishment is that any negative actions, thoughts, and words manifested by that enlightened Soul will reap negative consequences due to the Law of Cause and Effect. This Razor's Edge as it is called requires good self-discipline to walk because the higher a Soul climbs on the spiritual ladder toward the Godhead, the more quickly Spirit rushes to perform that Soul's wishes and desires, whether good or bad-intentioned. Bad-intentioned actions, thoughts, and words will rebound swiftly against a sender.

Chapter 12

JEFF JONES

My last view of Jeff Jones was from above. He was running along a dirt roadway between two rows of buildings before he stopped to peer ahead. Dressed in clothes that looked 1940 vintage, his light yellow brimmed hat matched his loose-fitting slacks. Beneath his tan jacket was a white shirt and dark suspenders. Built like a football fullback, Jeff was big and solid, maybe 6'2" tall and 210 pounds. Looking about 30 years of age, he wasn't ugly but almost. His large forehead topped with black hair gave him a sinister appearance. A male voice spoke to me from above, saying that Jeff had even taken advantage of his own grandmother before ending his life with a gun. I had been Jeff Jones in that lifetime.

Preceding this scene was another. While out of body floating in a light foggy sky, a male voice that I didn't recognize (the same voice as above) spoke not far away. Unable to hear clearly, I asked for the voice to speak again. A second time the voice came, telling me that I would be shown something about myself. I felt myself descend to a place where approximately 20 people, from early teens to maybe fifty years of age, were sitting together in a group. I dropped in from above and sat among them. Different males and females in the group then began telling me about the evils Jeff Jones had done to them in a former life. All had tried to make good in show business in that life, and all had stories to tell about how Jeff, an agent/manager, had cheated and taken advantage of them at every opportunity. They said Jeff was me in that lifetime. I asked about the time period and was informed the 1920's and years following.

Insight into my present life is what this vivid OOBE has given me. Past-life character patterns leave imprints in the subconscious mind which carry into future lives; this I have learned. Every karmic debt and injustice must someday be balanced out. My yesteryears in this lifetime are littered with failed friendships. My stock-market investments have turned sour. Jeff Jones didn't do well with people or money and neither have I.

Certainly I've had other bad former lives as well. All Souls go through a mix of good and bad in the reincarnation cycle. It is a relief to learn, however, that karmic debts can be repaid in the nonphysical worlds. With the help of Spirit, the Inner Master, or other spiritual guides, karma can be scrubbed clean through OOBE's and dreams, including those cloaked in symbols, if the message is understood subconsciously or consciously. "Reap what you sow" means learning from mistakes rather than "an eye or an eye". Spiritual growth is the result.

Summary

THE GAMEPLAN

While growing up I sometimes wondered about the meaning of life. What is life all about? What will the end be like, and is there anything after? Explanations from the Bible seemed farfetched. Not until my second conscious projection out of body did I realize that life's mysteries might be solvable before death. If people have inner bodies, evidently death is not the end. Here was precious knowledge, and something provable.

Other soul-travel adventures followed for me, revealing the existence of inner worlds with people and Godmen. Book-reading plus my OOBE's gave me new insights into the reasons for life and death.

I still remember a conversation here on Earth which involved a Catholic friend of mine. He asked me one day what my soul-traveling was good for, how it benefited me. The gist of his question was to demean soul travel as being either not possible, nonbeneficial, or perhaps evil. Knowing the religious devotion of my friend, I made no mention of religion or Godmen but instead simply stated that having proof of life after death is comforting to know. He looked at me and couldn't argue this, and I knew that his religion had not provided him with the same assurance, or what the afterlife might be like.

God's game of life, as I have come to understand and believe, is that all Souls must descend from the upper eternal heavens into the lower planes for the purpose of gaining spiritual wisdom. When sufficient spiritual advancement has been attained in the lower worlds, Soul

107

then returns to Its true home in the permanent heavens. The number of lifetimes spent in the lower planes accomplishing this will differ for each Soul.

Does Soul rest in peace and joy after returning to God's true heavens? No. Soul's reason for existence does not end upon regaining the upper heavens. The learning and climb toward God-consciousness continues for each enlightened Soul, a learning process which never ends.

The bad news about God's game of life is that the cycle of reincarnations in the lower planes will be long and arduous for every Soul. Ages of time can pass. But mistakes and hardships add up to learning which brings the good news. Each Soul will eventually win God's game of life and return to the eternal heavens. There are no exceptions. No evil Soul spends eternity in Hell. Gaining spiritual enlightenment means becoming a coworker with God. Sooner or later this divine fate awaits all Souls.

About the Author

Terrill Willson, author of "Dream Travel" and "How I Learned Soul Travel", held no interest in metaphysics while growing up. Not until adulthood did he learn about bilocation, from reading a book. Techniques described in that book soon helped Willson gain proof. It is possible for people to consciously leave their physical bodies. Nonphysical worlds do exist and can be visited before death.

Borrowing from his own soul-travel and dream-travel adventures, Willson tells a provocative story about life beyond the physical realm.